ARIZONA'S AMAZING TOWNS

South Mountain Park in Phoenix is the largest municipal park in the country and possibly in the world. This old tunnel is from a gold mine located in a remote canyon of South Mountain Park.

ARIZONA'S AMAZING TOWNS
From Wild West To High Tech

by
Richard Dillon

Four Peaks Press
P.O. Box 27401
Tempe, AZ 85285

iv

Library of Congress Catalog Card Number 92-070464

ISBN 0-9632377-0-5

Published by Four Peaks Press
P.O. Box 27401
Tempe, Arizona 85285

First edition — April 1992

Printed by Southwest Book Manufacturing — Tempe, Arizona

Dedication

To my parents —

Richard W. Dillon Sr. and Mary V. Peoples

From my father I acquired a love of Nature and the Great Outdoors of Arizona.

From my mother came a love of Reading and History.

The author with his parents in 1947.

Acknowledgements

The author wishes to thank the many writers whose work contributed to this book, many of whom are found in the Bibliography. The author suggests that readers who wish more in-depth information on Arizona towns start with the excellent books listed in the Bibliography. In addition, the author is indebted to many writers who have worked, often without bylines, for Arizona newspapers — including *Arizona Daily Star, Arizona Republic, Mesa Tribune, New Times, Arizona Gazette* and others.

The author also wishes to sincerely thank staff members at the Arizona Historical Society, Arizona Department of Library, Archives and Public Records, Hayden Library at Arizona State University, the University of Arizona Library, Tempe Public Library and especially the Arizona Room at the Phoenix Public Library.

Special thanks go to Susie Sato of the Arizona Historical Foundation who, over a period of many years, has always been most gracious and helpful. Thanks also to Don Ellis who reviewed the manuscript in its early stages. Anne Bassett and Dick Nearing have been most kind to allow me to use their excellent pen and ink drawings.

To my wife Mary Ann Van de Putte and our three daughters, Hope, Sage and Nora, I am eternally grateful. Not only did they help with typing, proof-reading and other menial tasks, but they had to suffer my frequent grumbling when things did not go quite the way I had hoped.

A writer by nature picks the brains of those he comes in contact with. This writer wants to thank friends, acquaintances and passersby who have made contributions both large and small. No doubt there are individuals who should be named here and perhaps they will forgive the author for this inadvertent omission.

Introduction

Many people say history is boring. Nothing could be further from the truth. History is not dull. It is filled with fascinating stories, incredible adventures and many events that are truly stranger than fiction. Arizona's history is as exciting as anyplace on earth.

Arizona is unique. Here the romance of the "Wild West" lives on beside the high tech world of nuclear weapons and semiconductor plants. *Arizona's Amazing Towns* brings all these elements together in a concise history of the most important, and most unusual, communities in the state. All the major cities are included. Several smaller towns were selected to spotlight significant aspects of life in Arizona such as the Mormon pioneer town of Snowflake, the Hopi Indian village of Oraibi and the retirement community of Sun City. Taken together these capsule histories give a general overview of Arizona past and present.

Arizona's Amazing Towns was never intended to be a Chamber of Commerce-type "everything is beautiful" hype. Instead it is a "warts and all" look at the people and places that shaped the state. Some readers may be offended because a "negative" side of a community is mentioned. The author only included such information because he felt it enhanced understanding. Other readers will no doubt complain because this or that was left out of the book. They will probably be right but not everything can be included in a book of this size. Whole volumes could be penned on even the smallest locale.

The author has had a lifelong love affair with Arizona. *Arizona's Amazing Towns* was written to inform and entertain the reader. It is hoped that the book will both increase the enjoyment of and foster a deeper appreciation of Arizona's rich heritage.

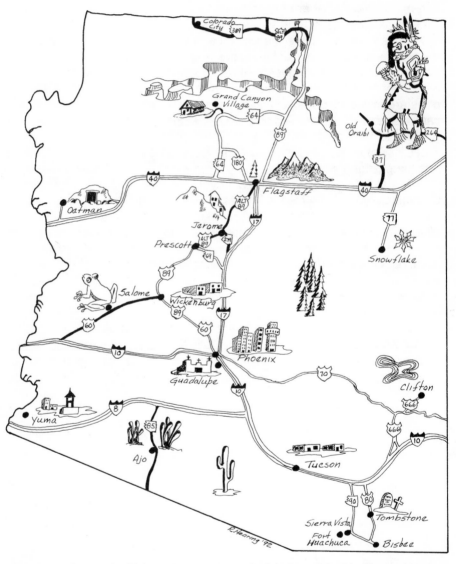

This map of Arizona by Richard Nearing shows the location of the 20 cities and towns covered in *Arizona's Amazing Towns*.

Table of Contents

Deforest Hall, better known as Dick Wick Hall, folk humorist of Salome in a youthful photo taken about 1900. *Credit — Arizona Historical Society*

SALOME

Home of Dick Wick Hall and His Famous Frog

"In the Southwest corner of Hell." That's where Salome founder and folk humorist Dick Wick Hall said you'd find his lonely desert town. Actually Salome is on the old Phoenix to Los Angeles highway (U.S. 60) about 50 miles east of the Colorado River.

Dick Wick Hall was a well-known "character" in Arizona in the early 1900's. His offbeat mind found humor in the hard everyday life on the desert. At Hall's Laughing Gas Station in Salome a sign beside the gas pumps read ... "Drive right up in your old bus and leave your money here with us."

In 1905 Dick Hall, a would-be real estate promoter, had high hopes for his new town. After all it did have a post office and a railroad stop. But Salome lies in the low desert where water is scarce and the heat can be horrendous. Rather than lie, Hall decided to promote his town with humor. He declared Salome a success. He said it had grown 100% per year or 19 people in 19 years.

Hall began to publish the *Salome Sun* ... "made with a Laugh on a Mimeograph." He gave it away free to travelers. Soon people from all over the country were talking about Salome and its fictitious residents like Chuckawalla Slim, Chloride Kate and the Reptyle Kid. *The Saturday Evening Post* even began to print his musings.

The *Salome Sun* would run basic news items. "It's Too Hot to Quarrel ... so the Ladies Aid Society didn't meet this week." The paper also waxed philosophic. "Out here in the Desert you Don't Need Much. And you Don't get much either and after a while you Don't Want Much." His spelling was a bit heavy with Capitals.

Hall claimed a pet rattlesnake named Lizzie. She was a Champion Jazz Soloist and even people who never took lessons would dance to her tunes. But Hall's most famous pet was the Salome Frog ...

> I'm Seven Years Old and I cannot Swim
> So don't Blame Me for Looking Grim
> When a Frog has to Carry a Big Canteen
> And Water his Back to keep it green ...

Salome's Greasewood Golf Course was unique and on the long side. The old prospector who laid it out confused yards with rods. The course was 6,429 rods long or just over 20 miles. Hall read a newspaper which reported a golfer had a score of 72, but he couldn't figure if "he made it in 72 hours or 72 days or used 72 balls going around."

Hall said on the Greasewood links, "Anything that don't move or is dead, like a Sand Wash or a Mesquite Thicket or a Dead Steer, we call a Bunker. Anything alive like a Rattlesnake or a Cow, we call a Hazard." One local player was Red Tatum from the Bermuda Ranch. "I got a letter from Red," Hall said. "He was out on the 11th hole and asked me to send him a Barrel of Water, a slab of Bacon, some beans and three dozen more balls."

Hall claimed the town was named for Mrs. Grace Salome Pratt, wife of a local railroad man. She removed her shoes to walk barefoot, but soon danced over the sizzling sands in pain. The town nickname was "Where She Danced." Most folks thought it referred to the Biblical Salome who danced for Herod and was presented with the head of John the Baptist on a silver platter.

Salome never did grow too much. The interstate highway to Los Angeles now bypasses the remote town. But Hall, who died in 1926 from kidney failure at age 49, is still remembered in his town. Every October the town holds Dick Wick Hall Days. And the local high school teams are called the Salome Frogs.

In the early years of this century the Laughing Gas Station in Salome was a popular stop for motorists enroute between Phoenix and Los Angeles. The station supplied all your automotive needs and dispensed a few laughs as well. *Credit — Arizona Department of Library & Archives*

OATMAN

A Dynamite Little Ghost Town

Often described as a "ghost town," Oatman is actually a lively little community famous for rich gold mines, obnoxious burros, and the wild west antics of some of its current residents.

The town is named for Olive Oatman, a 16-year-old white girl kidnapped by Indians along the Gila River Trail in 1851. One brother survived but the rest of her family died in the Oatman Massacre. Five years later Henry Grinnell heard of Olive from an Indian at Fort Yuma. He arranged for her release with threats of Army action and with gifts. Olive had been living with Mohave Indians at a spring near the present townsite.

Soldiers from Fort Mohave had prospected the region around Oatman in the 1860's. A man named John Moss reportedly took $240,000 from a gold pocket on the Moss Vein in 1864. But the Hualapai Indian Outbreak of 1866 caused the district to be completely abandoned. Apparently the area was "lost" for some 30 years.

Rich gold deposits lay within a mile of a busy wagon road but they remained undiscovered until 1896. A former Mexican Capitan, Jose Jerez, located the Gold Road Mine and the boom was on. Kingman merchant Henry Lovin had grubstaked Jerez with $12.50 in supplies and thus got half interest in the mine. It made Lovin fabulously rich but Jerez was less fortunate. He sold his share for $25,000 and soon spent all of it. Lovin continued to grubstake the impoverished Jerez until the old Mexican soldier died in 1906.

Many gold bearing veins were found and mines sprang up all over. When Oatman filed for a townsite in 1916 there were over 14 separate communities including Tent City, FortyNine Camp, Old Trails, Mazona, Times, and Gold Road. Oatman soon became the center of the district. Principal mines were the Tom Reed, Vivian, United Eastern, Snowball, Big Jim, Blue Ridge, Lazy Boy, Gold Dust, Midnight, and Sunnyside.

The World War One era was a stormy one. On July 7, 1917, the *Oatman News* ran this item ... "Constable Lacey arrested Peter Bacches for uttering treasonable and seditious sentiments against the United States on the streets of Oatman and took him to Kingman. Other arrests are threatened unless this kind of talk is muffled."

Government regulations in World War Two closed the Oatman gold mines although their heyday was long past. Another blow to the town came in 1951 when a new section of Route 66 bypassed the town. The next day six of Oatman's seven gas stations closed down. The population of Oatman dropped to about 40 in the 1960's but rebounded to over 200 in the 1980's.

Burros have always been a part of Oatman. In 1917 *Oatman News* reported ... "Burros are a menace to the town. They knock over trash cans, destroy property, and keep no regular hours and wake up miners trying to sleep." These burros are descendants of animals used by early day prospectors as pack animals.

In 1981 government agents began rounding up some 2000 burros that lived in the Black Mountains around Oatman. Besides making Oatman's main street an obstacle course, they threatened the endangered big horn sheep habitat. Some Oatman residents said the burros were town mascots and should be protected. But one disgruntled resident said they should kill the burros and then stuff them for the tourists.

Wild West antics continued to keep Oatman in the news in the 1980's. In 1981 town residents requested a permanent Deputy Sheriff to curb lawlessness. In 1983 a studio owned by local artist Jim King was destroyed by dynamite. King had painted a controversial mural that offended some citizens. In 1985 a Main Street business was bombed although no one was hurt in the explosion. In 1987 a dynamite bomb was found at the Old Trails Saloon and disarmed.

"It's a volatile little community," said a police detective from nearby Bullhead City. "A haven for people who live in the past," said another lawman. The local Justice of the Peace stated that "everyone has strapped on a sidearm."

Another controversy stirred Oatman in 1985 when a pyramid-shaped home was built overlooking the town. The builder was Herman Henning, a Danish health consultant and devotee of astrology and pyramid power. The pyramid is said to be the first significant building constructed in Oatman in 40 years. Some angry residents said it was a disgrace and threatened to blow it up.

Oatman, located 14 miles east of the Colorado River in Mohave County, remains a popular tourist attraction … despite local disputes over artistic taste and other human foibles.

Oatman burros are fat and sassy but always on the lookout for a free handout. *Credit —
Author*

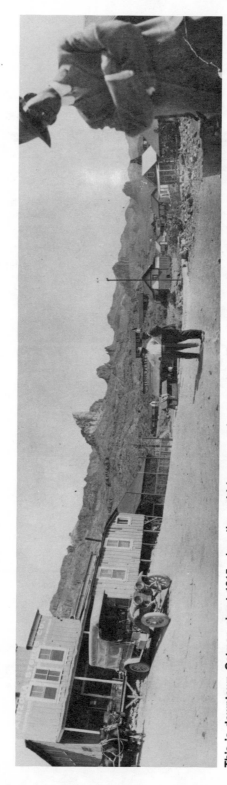

This is downtown Oatman about 1915 when the gold boom was just starting. The clever gentleman in the corner is Sidney P. Osborn, Arizona Secretary of State. The heavy gentleman in the center is George W.P. Hunt, Arizona's first and most popular governor. Hunt was re-elected seven times. He and Osborn are apparently on a statewide campaign trip. *Credit — Arizona Department of Library & Archives*

This 12-mule team freight wagon in Prescott in 1876 has just arrived with supplies from the Colorado River. Cargo was off-loaded from sailing ships in the Gulf of California. Then it was loaded onto paddle-wheel steamboats for the trip up the Colorado River. Prescott was distribution point for the gold mines, ranches and forts of northern Arizona before the railroads arrived. *Credit — Williscraft*

PRESCOTT

Arizona's All-American City

Prescott, the Mile High City, is a gold mining and cattle ranching center. For many years it was territorial capital of Arizona. Today Prescott retains many frontier roots, including the annual Fourth of July Rodeo, the "wild west" saloons of Whiskey Row, and the elm covered plaza of the Yavapai County Courthouse.

Gold fever attracted the first white men to Prescott. Captain Joseph Walker led an expedition of 30 gold prospectors here in the spring of 1863. They arrived at Granite Creek to find famous mountain man Pauline Weaver already living there. The Walker party fanned out and discovered rich gold-bearing gravels throughout the region. As more goldseekers rushed in, the Walker group adopted formal rules for the new mining district on May 10, 1863.

Pauline Weaver, Prescott's first resident, was a legendary fur trapper and guide who arrived in Arizona sometime before 1830. He may be the first "American" to settle in Arizona. An agent for the Hudson Bay Co., Weaver was an expert on Indian affairs. His mother was a Cherokee from Tennessee. Weaver tried to act as peacemaker between Yavapai Indians and gold miners, but his efforts were futile.

Pauline Weaver died at age 67 in 1867 and was first buried at old Camp Lincoln in Chino Valley. In 1929 Weaver's body was moved to Prescott and is now buried at the Sharlot Hall Museum. Weaver's Needle in the Superstition Mountains and two mining districts bear his name.

The town of Prescott was founded on May 30, 1864 at a citizens meeting on Granite Creek. It's said the townsite was surveyed by Robert Groom, who used a frying pan for a transit. The town was named for William H. Prescott, author of the classic history, *Conquest of Mexico.* Several streets bear names from his book — Cortez, Montezuma, Alarcon.

Fort Whipple was first established some 20 miles north of Prescott, but was too remote to protect the gold miners. In 1864 Fort Whipple moved to its present location just east of Prescott. The fort is named for General Amiel Whipple, who was killed at Chancellorsville during the Civil War. Whipple surveyed northern Arizona in the 1850's looking for a possible railroad route to California. Today Fort Whipple is a Veterans Hospital and many of the old buildings are still standing.

The Yavapai Indians inhabited the Prescott region for centuries before the gold miners arrived, but soon found themselves dispossessed. Often massacred by unscrupulous whites, the Yavapais fought back, killing isolated miners or ranchers and stealing livestock. The Army rounded up the hapless Yavapais and confined them at far-off San Carlos in eastern Arizona. Eventually the 15,000 or so Yavapais were reduced to some 200 survivors. Today the remaining Yavapai have a small reservation on the north side of Prescott.

President Abraham Lincoln created the Arizona Territory in 1863, and Prescott was selected as the capital. Tucson and other larger towns were overlooked because of Confederate sympathies. John Goodwin, the first Territorial Governor, convened the first legislature on September 2, 1864 in a log building. The structure was later destroyed in the big Prescott fire of 1900. In 1867 the capital moved to Tucson for 10 years. Prescott was again territorial capital from 1877 to 1889, at which time it was moved permanently to Phoenix.

Prescott was known as an "all-American" town from the beginning. There were very few Mexicans and no adobe style architecture. Unlike other early Arizona towns, Prescott was located in the mountains amid pine forests. Thus lumber was readily available and wood frame buildings were the rule.

Speaking of lumber ... an interesting historical note reveals that Virgil Earp ran a sawmill at Thumb Butte just west of Prescott. But the sometime lawman left for Tombstone (and the OK Corral) in 1879. Earp left town owing Goldwaters Store some $312.

Panning for gold was early Prescott's main industry. Rich placers were found at Lynx, Groom and Granite Creeks, as well as all along the upper Hassayampa River. With a little luck, prospectors could make fabulous sums of money. One man made $3,600 in 11 days working a rich deposit. (In those days gold prices were a fraction of today.) But prices of everything were sky-high. Mrs. Joe Ehle, the first white woman in Prescott, arrived with a pregnant cat. She soon sold a kitten to a lonely miner for an ounce of gold.

Hard rock gold mining has also been important to Prescott. The mines lie south of town throughout the Bradshaw mountain range. Many mines operated on and off from the late 1860's through the 1930's Depression era. Some small scale gold panning work is still done, often by weekend miners.

William O. O'Neill, better known as Buckey O'Neill, is Prescott's best known citizen. Regarded as a reckless gambler, O'Neill got his nickname from faro, the popular saloon game. Heavy betting on faro was called "bucking the tiger."

Controversial but quite popular, O'Neill came to Prescott in 1882 and was later elected mayor. He also served as sheriff of Yavapai County and was captain of the Prescott Blues, the local militia. O'Neill founded the stockmen's magazine, *Hoof and Horn,* and was editor of the Prescott newspaper, *Arizona Miner.* Buckey, always flamboyant, even printed a poem on the front page of the *Arizona Miner* to announce his wedding.

When the Spanish American War broke out, Buckey O'Neill was the first man to sign up. He joined Teddy Roosevelt's First U.S. Volunteer Cavalry, better known as the Rough Riders, and was made captain. Buckey O'Neill was killed in Cuba by a Spanish sniper on July 1, 1898, at age 38. Reckless to the end, Buckey had refused to take cover when the shooting started.

To commemorate Buckey O'Neill, citizens of Prescott commissioned a prominent artist, Solon Borglum, to design a large bronze sculpture. Borglum was America's first Cowboy Artist and was famous for equestrian works. He once worked as a cowboy in California and had studied veterinary medicine to learn horse anatomy. In 1907 the Buckey O'Neill statue was unveiled at the Courthouse Plaza where it still attracts admirers today. Solon's brother, Gutzon Borglum, was the artist who did the presidents' busts on Mount Rushmore. Prescott has other statues by Solon Borglum, including a "heroic" size piece at Yavapai College titled "Rough Rider."

The world's oldest rodeo began in Prescott on July 4, 1888. Juan Leyvas won the overall roping award, and Charlie Meadows took the bronc busting title that year. Meadows was a Prescott cowboy who had seen family members killed by Indians not far from town. As "Arizona Charlie Meadows," he became a western showman and performed with the Buffalo Bill Show.

The Fourth of July Rodeo became an annual Prescott event. It attracted local, state and national rodeo champions, as well as "western" celebrities. Cowboy movie star Tom Mix won the steer roping and bulldogging events in 1913 — before he found fame in Hollywood. Mix returned to Prescott to make movies at the American Horse Ranch and at Granite Dells. In 1933 humorist Will Rogers was Grand Marshall of the Rodeo Parade.

The Prescott Frontier Days Rodeo is still a rip-roaring affair. But in the old days … "cowboys would take possession of the town." Street dances were held on Whiskey Row and hard drinking and fighting were regular, but unscheduled events. The old-time rodeos would end with an afternoon horse race and an evening "hose race." In the days before full-time fire departments, teams of volunteer firemen would race to attach a water hose to a hydrant.

"Junior Bonner," a classic modern Western movie by Sam Peckinpah, spotlights the Prescott Rodeo. Filmed at the July 4, 1971 rodeo, it stars Steve McQueen as a rodeo champ with Ida Lupino and Robert Preston as his parents. The screenwriter, Jeb Rosenbrook, worked at nearby Orme Ranch School and was inspired by the annual rodeo. Many scenes were filmed on Whiskey Row and in the Palace Bar.

One early star of the Prescott Frontier Days Rodeo was local cowboy "Doc" Pardee, seen here about 1923. Pardee was a rancher and veterinarian who later served as "arena director" for the annual Prescott rodeo. Pardee's booming voice announced rodeo events as well as square dances in the days before microphones. *Credit — Arizona Historical Society*

Rodeo represents the importance of ranching to Prescott's economy. Ranching is the number one industry in the county as far as assessed tax valuations are concerned.

Whiskey Row has been located on Montezuma Street in Prescott for over 100 years. Saloons and brothels were clustered here in a red light district soon after the town was founded. Miners exchanged gold dust for booze and the temporary affections of ladies of the night.

On July 14, 1900 a fire destroyed all of Whiskey Row and most of Prescott's commercial district. Only two of the 35 saloons were spared. After the fire, saloons set up on the courthouse lawn and dance hall girls performed in the open air. Since the banks had also burned, the Sheriff acted as "treasurer" for the Whiskey Row saloonkeepers.

The Palace Bar opened in 1877 and was soon Whiskey Row's most famous establishment. The first building was completely destroyed in the 1900 fire but the massive mahogany bar was saved. Patrons carried the bar over to the courthouse plaza just across the street. The carved wood bar had come around the Horn on a clipper ship. Today the antique bar still impresses customers who patronize the Palace which was rebuilt on the original 1877 site. Frank Young, a black janitor, was the Palace Bar's longest running employee. He worked at the Palace from 1904 until his retirement in 1969. Since 1946 the Palace Bar has been owned by the Shell and Sally Dunbar family.

Morris Goldwater was selected Prescott's Man of the Century during the town's 100 year anniversary in 1963. Born in London in 1852, Morris Goldwater came to Prescott in 1876 to help run the family store. Morris had previously worked in Goldwaters stores in Phoenix and Ehrenburg. Morris Goldwater died in 1939 at age 87. At that time the Goldwaters stores had become Arizona's longest running mercantile establishment.

Morris Goldwater was a lifelong Democrat and served as Prescott mayor for 20 years. He also served on the Yavapai County Board of Supervisors and at the Arizona Legislature. His more famous nephew, Barry Goldwater, Arizona's long-time U.S. Senator, was the 1964 Republican nominee for president. Morris Goldwater is buried in the Masonic Cemetery in Prescott.

The Arizona Pioneers Home is a three-story brick building that sits on Murphy Hill overlooking downtown Prescott. It opened in 1911 to provide a home for impoverished pioneers to live out their last days in dignity. The 4.5 acre site was donated by Frank Murphy, builder of the railroad from Prescott to Phoenix. Then as now operating expenses came from lease fees paid by ranchers for use of state lands.

The original Pioneers Home had rooms for 40 men but no places for women. In 1916 an addition for women was built by W.C. Parsons, a Prescott miner who donated $30,000 to cover the costs. Today women residents outnumber men by three to one.

Until 1970 anyone living in Arizona for 35 years and at least 60 years old was eligible at no cost. Since 1970, Arizona Pioneers Home residents must be 70, a resident of Arizona for 30 years, and pay if they can afford it. To be admitted residents must be ambulatory but a 65 bed infirmary is available for those whose health fails. Today there are some 170 residents and a staff of 110 employees.

The average age is about 84. Only Alaska and Wyoming provide similar services to pioneers.

Sharlot Hall, a respected "Western" writer, was one of Arizona's best known women from the frontier era. Born in Kansas, Sharlot rode a horse down the Santa Fe Trail to Arizona at age 11. Her family came to Prescott in 1882 and settled at Orchard Ranch on Lynx Creek. As a child Sharlot's chores included milking cows, chopping wood, branding cattle and even panning for gold. Sharlot Hall only attended one semester of high school in Prescott but she later became the town's most literate pioneer.

Sharlot earned fame for poems, articles and essays on frontier Arizona life. It was something she knew firsthand. Her poem "Arizona" helped rally opposition against joint statehood with New Mexico. She was hired by Charles Lummis in 1901 to help staff his famous California magazine *Out West.* In 1909 Sharlot resigned from *Out West* to become the Arizona Territorial Historian. It was then that she began her extensive collection of historical artifacts.

In 1912 Sharlot Hall's mother died and Sharlot returned to Orchard Ranch to help care for her invalid father. When her father passed away in 1928, Sharlot moved into Prescott proper. She leased the old Governor's Mansion and started the museum that now bears her name. Sharlot Hall died in April 1943 at age 73.

The Sharlot Hall Museum is located at 415 W. Gurley. Museum buildings include the log cabin style Governors' Mansion built in 1864, the John C. Fremont House (1875), and the Coles Bashford House (1877). The Bashford House was moved to the museum grounds to make way for a fast food outlet. Exhibits and a gift shop are found in the Sharlot Hall Building (1934) which was built with Depression-era relief money.

Perched on the balcony of the world-famous Palace Bar on Prescott's Whiskey Row, Frontier Days revelers celebrate at the annual Fourth of July event. *Credit — Author*

Old Oraibi in the 1920's with a Hopi boy peeking out a window. The town is the oldest continuously inhabited community in the U.S. It was settled sometime before 1100 A.D. *Credit — McCulloch Brothers*

ORAIBI

Oldest Town in the United States

The Hopi village of Oraibi is the oldest town in the United States. It has been continuously inhabited since at least 1150 A.D. The Hopi, the western-most Pueblo Indians, live in a dozen compact villages on three jutting mesas high above the Painted Desert. Until recently, Oraibi was the largest and most important Hopi village. It's been described as a place "where ruins sit upon even more ancient ruins."

First recorded contact with the Hopi was in 1540 when Pedro de Tovar of the Coronado Expedition visited briefly seeking the legendary Seven Cities of Gold. Another Spanish expedition in 1583 found Oraibi to be the largest Hopi town.

Spanish missions were built at Oraibi and two other Hopi villages in 1628 but their reception was not sympathetic. A Hopi delegation traveled to New Mexico in 1650 to protest one Father Guerra, who had publicly beaten, then poured turpentine over a Hopi man, and burned the man to death. The priest accused the Hopi of idolatry because he followed traditional Hopi religion.

Spanish abuses led the Hopi to join New Mexico Indians in the Pueblo Revolt of 1680. Father Espelata and Father Santa Maria were killed at Oraibi and all Spanish mission buildings destroyed. The large mission beams were used in constructing Hopi religious centers or kivas. The Spanish soon returned to New Mexico but found remote Hopi-land more resistant.

Spanish missionaries did convince one Hopi village, Awatovi, to accept a Catholic Church but this led to the most tragic event in Hopi history. The Warrior Society of Oraibi, with Hopis from other villages, attacked Awatovi and killed all men in 1700. Women and children were divided between various villages and Awatovi was completely abandoned. This lesson to Hopi and Catholic Church alike effectively ended Spanish influence on the Hopi.

The next challenge to Hopi self-rule came when the U.S. government entered the picture in the 1880's. At this time Oraibi held half of all Hopi or about 1000 people. One reason for Oraibi's large population was that smaller villages were abandoned to increasing raids of marauding Navajo.

The U.S. government declared that all Hopi children must attend schools but most Hopi resisted especially at Oraibi. In 1890 soldiers from Fort Defiance captured 104 school age children and forcibly took them away to school. Again the next year Col. Corbin and four troops of black soldiers with Navajo scouts threatened the entire village of Oraibi with machine guns because children were kept out of school. This continued for many years.

Belle Axtell Kolp, a teacher at Oraibi in 1903, resigned to protest treatment of Hopi by Indian Agent Charles Burton. Mrs. Kolp said Burton used Navajo police to round up children in the dead of winter nights. Burton even forcibly cut hair of adult Hopi males who maintained traditional ways.

In 1906 a dispute divided Oraibi between traditional Hopis called "hostiles" and progressive Hopis called "friendlies." The "hostiles" were led by Yukioma and the "friendlies" were led by Tewaquaptewa. The dissension was so great that civil war seemed likely. Yukioma decided to settle this by drawing a line in the sand. He told the "friendlies" if they could push him over the line, he and his followers would leave Oraibi forever. With his people behind him, Yukioma was pushed back and forth but finally the "friendlies" pushed him over the line.

Yukioma led his followers out of Oraibi and founded the new village of Hotevilla, eight miles to the north. Hotevilla remains the most traditional Hopi village. Yukioma was often imprisoned by U.S. authorities for his continued intransigence.

The Hopi Tribal Council was introduced in 1936 and has been a point of dispute between traditional and progressive Hopis ever since. Some Hopi claim the vote to approve the Council was fraudulent since hostile Hopis refused to participate in the election. Others say they voted yes thinking it meant they'd retain their lands.

Traditional Hopis refuse to recognize or obey Tribal Council actions. They prefer the old leadership system where each village acted as an autonomous city-state. Each Hopi village has a Kikmongwi or chief that is selected by clan membership and acts as a spokesman or interpreter of current events. In addition, a village council made of leaders of important Hopi sodalities or social organizations, acts as village government.

The Oraibi chief or Kikmongwi for most of this century has been Tewaquaptewa. After the famous tug-of-war which split Oraibi in 1906, Tewaquaptewa was forced to leave Oraibi by U.S. government order. He and his family were sent to the Sherman Institute, a Indian training school in Riverside, California. Tewaquaptewa was supposed to learn American ways. But in 1910, when he was allowed to return to Oraibi, he had changed from a friendly to a hostile Hopi.

Tewaquaptewa soon forced all Christian Hopis, mostly Mormon or Mennonite, out of Old Oraibi. New Oraibi or Kiakochomovi, below the mesa, was founded by these outcasts. Described as bitter and a tyrant, he also drove other Hopis out and many went to Moenkopi village. By the time Tewaquaptewa died in 1960, Old Oraibi had declined dramatically with perhaps 10% of its old population.

After Tewaquaptewa's death, a dispute arose over his successor. The traditionals recognized Mina Lanza, a woman of the Parrot clan. The Tribal Council recognized a Hopi man named Myron. Mina Lanza and her husband John, who raised 12 children together, sometimes shared duties as Kikmongwi. John Lanza, as head of the Badger clan, would take Mina's place in ceremonies that forbid women. When Mina Lanza died in 1978, Oraibi and the Hopi traditionals lost a vigorous voice for old Hopi ways.

The Hopi have been called the "most thoroughly religious people in the world." Public ceremonies are common between December, when the Kachinas arrive, and July when they return home to San Francisco Peaks. Kachinas are animalistic spirits or generalized ancestor figures rather than "gods." There are 30 primary Kachinas and several hundred lesser ones. Kachina dolls, carved from cottonwood root and brightly painted, are popular crafts sold to tourists and highly valued by collectors.

Religious activities center around the "kiva," a large underground room where the Kachinas stay while in Hopi villages. Two long ladder poles rising out of bare ground mark the entrance to these mysterious chambers. Kivas also function as a male lodge in the matrilocal Hopi society where women traditionally own the houses. Men often stay in the kivas to relax, work on crafts and prepare ceremonial rituals.

The Hopi Indian Reservation is located some 90 miles northeast of Flagstaff. It is completely surrounded by the sprawling Navajo Indian Reservation. Visitors to Oraibi should check with local Hopis to determine whether the village is currently open to outsiders.

Entrance sign at Old Oraibi in 1972. The sign reflects the division between Hopi factions. Some Hopi welcomed white visitors while others obviously did not. This sign was torn down and replaced on several occasions. *Credit — Author*

Yuma was the principal steamboat port for the Colorado River. Here the steamboat Gila is tied up at the end of Main Street in 1898. Yuma steamboats plied up and down the river after receiving Arizona bound cargo from sailing ships docked in the Gulf of California.
Credit — Arizona Historical Foundation

YUMA

Steamboat Port on the Colorado River

Paddlewheel steamboats, flat-bottom barges and riverboat captains are not usually associated with Yuma. But the image is accurate. For 50 years Yuma was homeport for several steamboats that cruised the Colorado River carrying cargo to mining towns and Army forts. Unlike any other Arizona town, Yuma was created because it had too much water.

Two mighty rivers converge just above Yuma — the Colorado (1450 miles long) and the Gila (630 miles long). Moreover, two rocky hills force the river to narrow here. As a result Yuma is the best place to cross the lower Colorado. Today Fort Yuma occupies the western hill, and Yuma Territorial Prison sits atop the eastern knoll.

This area was home to the Yuman or Quechan Indians since prehistoric times. Life was "easy" along the lush river. The Yumas ate fish, grew vegetables in the floodplain and harvested natural foods. Most important was the mesquite bean which was pounded into flour. The Yumas used wood rafts or giant pottery jars to float across the river.

The Yumas got their name from the Spanish word "humo" or smoke. The Yumas often set huge fires along the river. One historian said they were seeding rainclouds with smoke particles. It is more likely they were just practicing slash-and-burn agriculture.

The first European at Yuma was Spanish Capitan Alarcon who sailed up the Colorado River in 1540. The Spanish knew the Yuma Crossing was important but the warlike Yumas were always unfriendly. Padre Kino visited Yuma about 1700, as did Padre Sedelmair in 1744. Capitan Juan de Anza crossed here on his way to colonize California in 1776. But only the zealous Padre Garces came to stay.

Fray Hermengildo Garces was the last great Catholic missionary in the Southwest. After extensive travels he settled at Yuma in 1779 with instructions to secure the strategic site for the Spanish Crown. He soon set up two missions including one on the west side of Yuma Crossing.

Trouble brewed as the Spanish colonists abused the Yumas and took away their best lands. Priests forced the Indians to become Christian and public whippings were common. Even Chief Palma, who originally welcomed Garces, turned against him. The last straw came when California bound colonists turned their livestock into the mesquite forests to feed on the ripe beans. Some Yumas tried to save their food supply and were brutally shot down by the Spanish.

The Yuma Massacre occurred in July 1781. The Indians killed every Spanish man in the region, including Garces, three other priests, and about two dozen soldiers. About 50 men were killed but no women or children were harmed. The Yumas later released 48 captives. The Spanish left Yuma never to return and the crossing remained in the hands of the Yumas.

The California Gold Rush of 1849 brought the first American settlers to Yuma. One group was led by John Glanton, a professional Apache scalp hunter who was run out of Mexico for selling scalps of friendly Indians. Glanton and his gang of cutthroats operated a ferryboat and amassed a small fortune over-charging immigrants. But Glanton made the mistake of mistreating the Yuma Indians and even murdered the white operator of their ferry. The Yumas killed Glanton and a dozen of his men. It's said that over $60,000 disappeared.

Fort Yuma was built on the California side in 1851 to make peace at the crossing. It was constructed on the site of the old Garces mission. To communicate with the Yumas, Major Heintzelman appointed Pasqual "Chief of the Yumas." Pasqual served in that position for many years. Rations and equipment for Fort Yuma came by sea and it soon became the main depot for supplying all other Arizona forts.

Yuma's picturesque riverboat days were ushered in by the "Uncle Sam," a 65-foot sternwheeler. It was the first steamboat on the Colorado River. Captain Turnbull brought the vessel up river from the Gulf in 1852. But two years later it ran aground and sank. It was replaced by the "General Jesup," which unfortunately was destroyed soon after when its boiler exploded.

The "Colorado," a 120-foot sternwheeler, began plying the river in 1855 and remained on the scene for many years. Another early steamboat was the "Explorer" in which Lt. Ives explored the Colorado River in 1858. Other Yuma-based steamboats were the 140-foot "Cocopah," and the "Mojave," which could carry almost 200 tons of freight.

The first commercial building in what is now the city of Yuma was built by a prostitute nicknamed the "Great Western." Sarah Bowman came to Fort Yuma in 1853 to cook for the officers. Within a year she had constructed a large adobe building across the river from the fort. Her establishment was a combination bar, restaurant and brothel. It was located at First and Main, where the Valley Bank is now.

A notorious "camp follower," Sarah was with Gen. Taylor's army in Mexico in 1846. She became famous for her courage during the artillery bombardment of Fort Brown. Standing six feet tall and full-bodied, Sarah was dubbed the Great Western after the large ocean-going steamship of the same name. It's said this "Amazon" hooker really did have a heart of gold. When she died at Yuma in 1867, the soldiers gave her a military style funeral. Fort Yuma was abandoned in the 1880's and her body was removed with the others. The Great Western now lies in the Army cemetery at the San Francisco Presidio.

The Yuma Territorial Prison (1875-1909) is a part of Arizona folklore. The original cells were cut from solid rock on Prison Hill. Troublemakers were sent to the Snake Den, a dark cave-like cell. Some say guards dropped snakes or scorpions down the air vent to torment those in solitary confinement.

The prison was called a "hellhole" but in some ways it was an enlightened place. Yuma Prison had one of the first libraries in the state. There were even classes for illiterates. In 1885 big electric fans were installed to cool the cellblocks in summer. Most prisoners spent only one or two years at the prison. Similar crimes draw much longer sentences these days. For example, Buckskin Frank Leslie, a well-known Tombstone killer, was sentenced to life but was pardoned after just seven years.

The best known prisoner was Pearl Hart, a Benson dancehall girl who robbed a stagecoach with her boyfriend. She was sentenced to five years in 1899 but was released two years later. Some say prison authorities released her early because she was a troublemaker. Others say she was pregnant and released to avoid

The Yuma Territorial Prison once housed Arizona's most dangerous outlaws, but today it is a popular tourist stop operated by the State Parks Department. *Credit — Author*

scandal. Pearl went to New York and performed in vaudeville for awhile. Then she dropped out of sight. Her chrome-plated .44 pistol is on display at the Arizona Historical Society in Tucson.

One myth says that no one ever escaped from the Yuma Prison. Actually 26 men fled the prison never to be recaptured. Eight men were killed trying to escape. A total of 3069 prisoners were held at Yuma — 29 of them were women. Some 113 inmates died there including Phoenix founder Jack Swilling.

The prison closed in 1909 and for five years the empty buildings were used as classrooms for the Yuma High School. This led to the Yuma High teams being nicknamed the Criminals. They still sport that title today. In the 1920's the deserted prison grounds were used as a hobo jungle, as it was convenient to the railroad. Today the prison is a popular State Historic Park.

Southern Pacific Railroad reached Yuma in September 1877 laying tracks from Indio. To avoid opposition in Yuma, the railroad bought out the local steamboat company (Colorado Steam Navigation). However Congress had granted the southern rail route across Arizona to the Texas Pacific Railroad. Construction of the railroad bridge was ordered stopped. The crews worked secretly at night and soon finished the bridge. Troops were brought in and the bridge was forcibly closed for a time. Finally President Hays granted Southern Pacific the right to enter Arizona and the railroad pushed on toward Tucson.

A special drawbridge was built to allow steamboats to travel up and down the river. For many years this revolving drawbridge was a favorite "ride" for Yuma residents. Adults and kids alike would climb aboard the swinging bridge whenever a boat passed.

Laguna Dam was built just north of Yuma in 1909. It brought a golden age of agriculture to the area. However, farmers on the Arizona side of the river had to wait for water until 1912, when a giant siphon was completed. The Yuma Siphon was a 965-foot-long tunnel that carried irrigation water underneath the Colorado River to canals south of Yuma.

Yuma was the Marriage Capital of Arizona in the 1930's. This distinction resulted from California's "gin marriage law" which required a three-day waiting period so couples could "sober up" before tying the knot that binds. In 1940 Yuma recorded 17,000 marriages but only had 5,000 residents. Movie stars like Tom Mix, Erroll Flynn, Jean Harlow, and Buster Crabbe had quicky marriages in Yuma.

Yuma has long been the brunt of jokes about its scorching summer temperatures. Kit Carson described the area as ... "so desolate and God-forsaken that a wolf could not make a living on it." The *Sentinel* newspaper said Yuma ... "is the hottest place on earth. Americans stand in the Colorado River half the day and keep drunk the rest of the time to avoid death by melting." Another tale says a soldier from Fort Yuma died and went to Hell. But the soldier found it too chilly there and returned to Yuma for his blankets. Arizona humorist Bob Boze Bell has continued this ribbing. He says ... "to imagine life in Hell all you need is a sense of Yuma." It is "the town that winter forgot" with "year round blast furnace ambiance." And "Yuma-ke me sweat."

Today Yuma has a population of some 50,000. Agriculture is the main industry, but the Marine Corps Air Station is also an important factor in the local economy. It is county seat for Yuma County. For some 15 miles southwest of Yuma, Arizona is divided from Mexico by the Colorado River. Yuma is an important border crossing for travel to and from Mexico.

WICKENBURG

Dude Ranch Capital of the World

In the fall of 1863, German immigrant Henry Wickenburg was prospecting for gold in Indian country. In the distance he saw a white quartz hilltop sparkling in the sun with a black vulture circling ominously above it. On closer inspection, Wickenburg found free gold among the quartz crystals. Chunks of free gold. The Vulture, perhaps Arizona's richest gold mine, had been discovered.

One problem was lack of w... at the Vulture Mine. To process the gold ore Wickenburg needed water. Fifteen miles away was the Hassayampa River and a Yavapai Indian village called Pumpkin Patch. Wickenburg ran the Indians off and set up a primitive Spanish-style mill and smelter. Soon the boom town of Wickenburg sprang to life around the gold smelting works.

Wickenburg worked the rich Vulture ore for a few years and then sold out to Benjamin Phelps of New York for $85,000. He got $20,000 in cash and retained a 20% interest in the Vulture Mine. However the deal went sour and Wickenburg spent the rest of his life in an unsuccessful attempt to collect the balance owed him.

Wickenburg built a model farm on the Hassayampa River with a large peach orchard and many acres of grain fields. However, more bad luck struck in 1890 when the Walnut Grove Dam failed. The dam, 18 miles north of Wickenburg, sent a wall of water 40 feet high rushing down the Hassayampa River. It is said that a messenger was sent to warn residents below the dam that it was about to collapse. But the messenger reputedly got drunk at the first saloon and never completed his mission. Some 63 bodies were recovered but many more died in the disaster.

Henry Wickenburg's farm was also destroyed. Wickenburg survived but the 70-year-old man became embittered and claimed to lose all interest in living. However, the tough old buzzard held on another 15 years, living in poverty in a tunnel, just outside the town that bears his name. In 1905 Henry Wickenburg shot himself to death with his Colt revolver.

The Wickenburg Massacre in 1871 created a stir throughout the Territory and the country. The stage was only six miles from Wickenburg on the road to the Colorado River when it was ambushed by nine men in Army issue overcoats. Six men including the stage driver and Frederick Loring were killed. The death of Loring, a prominent Boston writer who'd recently been with the Wheeler Survey, increased the outrage and attention the deed received nationally. A Miss Mollie Shepard and a Mr. Kruger survived by fleeing on foot.

Controversy raged over who was responsible for the massacre ... Indians from the Date Creek Reservation or Mexicans and Americans disguised as Indians. Miss Shepard, a "courtesan" in Prescott was known to be carrying $15,000 in gold as well as valuable jewelry. Her bag was one of few opened by the killers. This plus the fact that no horses or ammunition were taken tended to support the theory of a non-Indian raiding party. However, Army troops were sent to Date Creek and a number of Indians were killed in a campaign that followed.

In the early 1870's the Vulture Mine closed down and the fortunes of Wickenburg declined with it. The Vulture Mine was one of the richest ever seen in Arizona. A couple hundred men were employed at the mine and the mill in town. The population in 1870 was 460 but in 1883 only about 50 people remained in town. From 1875 until about 1900 Wickenburg was described as a "ghost town" with over 100 empty homes and businesses.

Things perked up in 1895 when a railroad line from Phoenix to Prescott came through town. In 1909 Wickenburg incorporated as a city. The first city ordinance passed forbid women from wearing men's clothes and vice versa. It's still in place today. Other ordinances declared outhouses must be at least eight feet deep and that horses and mules in town must be tied to "permanent" fixtures.

Wickenburg has been called "The Dude Ranch Capital of the World." The first ranch was the Remuda, a 16,000 acre spread that opened in 1925. It had an airstrip and ranch school for its well-heeled patrons. During the 1930's three-day rodeos attracted thousands to the ranch. Well-known British author J.B. Priestly penned his famous book "Midnight on the Desert" while staying at the Remuda. The ranch was owned by Jack and Sophie Burden until 1969 when it was sold to Glen Berry.

Today a few guest ranches remain. The Kay El Bar was homesteaded in 1916 by Romaine Lowdermilk, a popular "western" singer, and opened for guests in 1927. Rancho de los Caballeros was opened in 1948 by Dallas Gant and also boasted an airstrip. The Flying E, a working ranch with 17,000 acres, was started in 1948 by George and Vi Wellick.

Wickenburg's location beside the Hassayampa River was source of much mirth. Hassayampa is an Indian word meaning "smooth running water" but other Indians

Horse corrals at the Remuda Guest Ranch near downtown Wickenburg. The Remuda, started by Jack Burden in 1925, hosted many famous guests and became the premier ranch in the Dude Ranch Capital of the World. Three-day rodeos were held here in the 1930's. *Credit — Author*

called it the "upside down" river since it flowed mostly underground. However, the most famous story concerns a magical quality attributed to the water. This old poem by Andrew Downing recalls the Hassayampa River's reputation …

> Those who drink its water bright
> Red man, white man, boor or knight
> Girls or women, boys or men
> Never can tell the truth again

Another version states … "If you drink its water, you will never tell the truth, own a dollar or leave Arizona." Local mining men resented this legend saying it prevented investors from looking seriously at area mines.

Today Wickenburg has a population of about 4,000. Among its current residents are the Quayle family, relatives of Vice President J. Danforth Quayle and heirs to the Pulliam newspaper empire which owns the *Arizona Republic* and *Phoenix Gazette*.

This drawing by Jerome artist Anne Bassett highlights the old mining town's fabulous views. Jerome clings to the steep slopes of Cleopatra Mountain and offers views of the Verde Valley, the red rocks of Sedona and in the far distance the snow-capped San Francisco Peaks.

JEROME

From Boom Town to Ghost Town to Art Colony

Overlooking the beautiful Verde Valley, Jerome is a picturesque mine town that clings precariously to the lofty slopes of Cleopatra Mountain. Directly underneath Jerome is a virtual honeycomb of abandoned mine shafts and tunnels that reach thousands of feet into the mountain. Once one of the richest mining towns in the world, Jerome almost became a ghost town when the mine closed. But today Jerome has been reborn as a refuge for people seeking an alternative lifestyle.

First mention of the Jerome mines occurred in 1582 when a Spanish expedition found an Indian turquoise mine at this site. However, no Spanish mining took place due to the Apache threat. Sometime in the 1870's Americans opened several small mines here but production lagged due to a lack of capital for expansion.

The United Verde Copper Co. was founded in 1882 when F.F. Thomas took over 11 adjoining claims. A New York financier, Eugene Jerome, became secretary of United Verde and the town was named after him. The United Verde took out rich silver and copper ore but closed down, and put out a "For Sale" sign, when ore quality declined in late 1884.

Enter William A. Clark, a small red-haired mine owner from Montana. Clark was already quite wealthy when he bought the United Verde in 1887. But the Jerome mine made Clark one of the 12 richest men in America. He was also known as one of the least philanthropic. Described as ruthless and cruel, Clark was listed as one of 100 capitalists who ruled the United States. In 1901 it is said he bribed his way into the U.S. Senate by paying out $1,000,000 to various interests in Montana.

Just how much money Clark made from the United Verde is not known. Clark was absolute ruler of his empire. There were no public shares, no partnerships, no bonds and no mortgages. Thus he had no need for a public accounting of his profits. Clark was very secretive and even sent coded messages to his United Verde mine managers.

In 1893 Clark built a narrow gauge railroad, the United Verde and Pacific, to link Jerome with the Santa Fe rail system. The 27-mile route was described as a corkscrew line with 187 curves and 28 bridges. In 1912 Clark built a new smelter complex in the valley below Jerome and called the town Clarkdale. Clark often parked his private railroad car in Clarkdale during his inspection trips. Another railroad spur ran directly into the underground United Verde mine. The famous Hopewell Tunnel, a 6,600-foot-long affair, linked the railroad to the 1,000 foot level inside the mine.

Clark's United Verde Mine was not the only one in Jerome. George Hull was a Jerome merchant who bought up "fractions" or small plots between the larger mining claims. In 1899 Hull formed the United Verde Extension (UVX) and began to sell shares. Rawhide Jimmy Douglas (his father was president of Phelps Dodge), took an option on the UVX in 1912. Phelps Dodge declined to buy the UVX because of Clark's control of Jerome. Ironically the elder Douglas had turned down a chance to buy the original United Verde before Clark bought it. But in 1914 Douglas's mining crew struck a huge deposit of 45% copper ore.

The United Verde Smelter at Jerome before 1915. Note the workers quarters perched on the hillside to the left of the smelter. In 1915 the smelter was moved to Clarkdale because the smelter sat above the underground mine. It was feared the immense weight would cause a cave-in. *Credit — Arizona Collection ASU*

However, lawsuits tied up production. Hull, an elderly man, was grilled by lawyers for several hours on the witness stand. This apparently contributed to his death the next day (October 26, 1916). A deal between United Verde and UVX divided up Hull's property amongst themselves. By the time the UVX Mine closed in 1938 it had paid over $55,000,000 in dividends, mainly to the Douglas family.

William Clark had vowed to keep the rich United Verde Mine in his family forever. But Clark died in 1925 and his sons died in 1933 and 1934. One son was killed in an airplane crash at Clarkdale while his wife watched from the family mansion. The remaining heirs sold the United Verde to Phelps Dodge in 1935 for about $20,000,000 ... a bargain insiders said. The purchase included the Clarkdale smelter and 90,000,000 pounds of copper bars ready for delivery.

Phelps Dodge operated the United Verde Mine until 1953 when they shut down operations. From 1887 til 1953 the United Verde Mine produced over 2½ billion pounds of copper, 50,000,000 ounces of silver and a million ounces of gold. These totals do not include production from the UVX or other local mines.

"Jerome Burns Again" was a common headline in Arizona newspapers in the 1890's. One sarcastic headline read ... "Entire Business District of 24 Saloons and 14 Chink Restaurants Destroyed." In 1897 an irate prostitute at Japanese Charley's "Sporting House" threw a kerosene lamp at a customer. The roaring fire soon spread through Jerome. Firefighting efforts were hampered by saloon owners who said "all the whiskey you want for carrying it off." Men left the fire lines to get drunk for free. An inadequate water supply, cramped streets and tinderbox wood buildings made Jerome especially susceptible to devastating fires.

One Jerome fire burned out of control for decades. However, this fire was deep underground in the mine. In 1894 the fire began in a sulfide stope or excavation area. It soon spread to support timbers and other mine works. Miners could not extinguish the fire and had to seal off burning sections of the mine. Reports say this fire was still smoldering into the early 1940's.

Another fire devastated William Clark's pet project. In 1900 Clark built the "finest hostelry in Arizona," the massive five-story, 200-room Montana Hotel. The dining room had magnificent copper chandeliers and seated 400. Designed to house United Verde employees and business guests, the Montana Hotel featured its own butcher shop, bakery, barber shop and laundry. It was built of local stone and Clark claimed proudly that it was "fireproof." But in 1915 the Montana Hotel burned to the ground, never to be rebuilt. Foundation stones are still visible north of town near the open pit mine.

In 1918 Jerome's pro-company newspaper reported that a "Mexican Uprising" had been defeated by local lawmen. A man named Hernandez, "his courage fortified with a marijuana cigaret," supposedly led a group from Mexican Gulch into the town with the intent of taking it over. A gunbattle ensued in which the Chief of Police and a deputy marshall were wounded. A mine watchman and Hernandez were killed. Other reports said that two groups of lawmen actually shot up each other by mistake. The special deputy that killed Hernandez was later fired for misconduct in making another arrest. Three Mexican co-conspirators were released for lack of evidence against them.

Jerome became known as a "art colony" after the mine closed in 1953 and the population plummeted to "ghost town" levels. The most famous Jerome artist, Lew Davis, was actually a native born in Jerome in 1910. Davis was a semi-abstract painter who specialized in somber scenes of life in Arizona's mine towns. His work is found in the Phoenix Art Museum and in the Valley Bank Collection. He died near Scottsdale in 1979.

Today many resident artists continue to make Jerome a flourishing artistic community. Two of the best known are the Bassetts. Don Bassett makes whimsical metal sculptures from "found" objects. His daughter, Anne Marie Bassett, is a painter and draftsman whose pen and ink drawings document historical Jerome buildings. Her work has appeared in *Arizona Highways.* Anne is also the "curator" of Jerome's open-air Art Park where she can be found on most weekends.

On the Jerome music scene a progressive rock band called Major Lingo has attracted a statewide following. Major Lingo has a unique sound that embraces folk elements with a touch of 1960's psychedelic. They make use of a "cowboy" slide guitar that produces sounds seldom heard in a country/western band.

One of Jerome's most unusual stories concerns Father Juan Gorostiaga (Father John), a Catholic priest of the Claretian Order. Father John first came to Jerome in 1927 and remained there until his death 42 years later at age 78.

On June 8, 1979 several Jerome residents including Mayor Dick Martin and Glenn Baisch gathered outside the Sacred Family Church. They decided to break into Father John's private rooms. The old priest, who usually sat outside everyday with his pet dogs, had not been seen for some time. Once inside they found Father John stuck between his bed and a wall in a weak and dazed condition. When the ambulance arrived, the old man refused to leave and had to be strapped to a chair to be taken to the hospital. It was soon discovered why Father John would not leave. His rooms were filled to overflowing with many thousands of dollars. This cash had been accumulated by Father John during his many years as Jerome's sole priest.

Silver coins were found in dozens of cardboard boxes, milk cartons and even in thermos bottles. Six thousand dollars were found in a cut-out book. A local church member, Alfredo Gutierrez, was appointed caretaker. The priest died soon afterwards. Just how much money was discovered has been a subject of some controversy. A couple of months before two unidentified men fled the church one night after being discovered. They left behind some $4700 in silver coins scattered on the church floor. Father John's house was ransacked the day he died and it burned to the ground mysteriously the next day. Catholic Bishop Rausch later stated that $27,000 was with the diocese and another $43,000 was put in a bank account. This money was set aside for church restoration.

"The main industry in Jerome is not tourism, it's drugs," a bitter Jerome resident once claimed to a visiting reporter. This reputation has grown ever since hippies began moving to Jerome in the 1960's. However, the extent of the problem is in some dispute.

In 1983 Glenn Baisch was arrested for growing marijuana in his backyard in Jerome. His next door neighbor was a Jerome city policeman. However, the illegal weed was discovered by helicopter. Baisch was first charged with having 980 pounds of pot but this weight included soil and rocks attached to plant roots. The final dry weight was approximately 50 pounds. Baisch, a long-time Jerome resident, was convicted but continued to live in the town.

Rumors of Jerome police compliance with the drug culture often surfaced. City council members reportedly told local police to ignore "victimless" crimes. State and

High House in Jerome sometimes appears ready to tumble down the mountainside — as some nearby buildings actually did a few years back. High House is located across the street from the popular House of Joy restaurant, a one-time brothel. *Credit — Author*

federal narcotics agents began to distrust Jerome police officials and often went around them to make busts. Long-time Police Chief Ron Ballatore was forced to resign after a massive raid on the town.

At 5:00 a.m. on October 11, 1985 over 50 agents with the Arizona Department of Public Safety and U.S. Drug Enforcement Agency descended on Jerome. To signal coordinated raids on numerous homes, the agents rang the Jerome fire bell. Many locals are volunteer firemen and everyone in town fears fire. Dazed and fearful residents scrambled to find the non-existent fire while agents burst into the homes of suspected drug dealers. This action by the drug agents left many Jerome residents outraged at the callous behavior.

The people arrested became known as the Jerome 24 and a Defense Fund was set up in their behalf. Only 100 pounds of marijuana were found and of that total 75 pounds were found at one house. Anne Bassett, a city council member, had to resign her post and was later sentenced to 30 days for selling a small amount of marijuana. The informer was an ex-convict who was promised immunity for other serious crimes he had committed. However, he disappeared soon after and some of the arrested had charges dropped.

"Picking on Jerome is an annual event," one local artist said. Most residents feel the small scale marijuana trade is really insignificant. They believe harassment for living a counter-culture lifestyle is the real problem.

Glenn Baisch was not one of the Jerome 24 but he was arrested for a second time in 1987. This time he was growing a marijuana patch in the mountains outside of town. Current Arizona law states that a second time offender must be sentenced to a mandatory 28 years in prison. In other words, the judge is given no discretion in these cases. Out on bail and very despondent, Baisch committed suicide rather than face the rest of his life in prison. Jerome residents held a memorial service for Baisch and his death became a symbol for the town.

SNOWFLAKE

Pioneer Morman Town

Mormons from Utah began colonizing Arizona in the 1870's in an effort to expand their "Zion." Snowflake was one of the first Mormon towns and it remains an important center for the religion. Snowflake is located 30 miles south of Holbrook on Silver Creek, a tributary of the Little Colorado River.

Mormon land agent William J. Flake found a suitable townsite on the old Stinson Ranch. He arranged to buy the ranch from James Stinson for $12,000 worth of Utah cattle in 1878. However, the Mormons had to pay for the land a second time. The land had been given to the Santa Fe Railroad by the U.S. government as compensation for building the expensive rail line to California. Santa Fe sold the land to the Aztec Land and Cattle Company, better known as the Hashknife Ranch. The Mormons agreed to pay $4.50 an acre for seven sections of land and finally obtained a clear title in 1889.

The town name has a quaint origin. Erastus Snow was the Mormon Apostle who directed the Mormon colonists from his home in St. George, Utah. He was known as the Field Marshall of Arizona colonization. Snow met with William Flake on the old Stinson Ranch and the two men cleverly decided to combine their names for the new town.

William Flake was legendary in the Little Colorado River region of eastern Arizona. One friend suggested this simple epitaph ... "He bought ranches. He made towns." In addition to Snowflake, William Flake purchased land for the Mormon towns of Showlow, Taylor, Shumway, Eagar, Concho and Nutrioso.

In 1884 William Flake and six other prominent Mormons were indicted for polygamy. Flake spent several months in the infamous Territorial Prison in Yuma but continued the marriages after his release. Polygamy was a common practice in the early Mormon Church. Leader Brigham Young had many wives. However, this practice was a source of resentment toward the religion and eventually the Mormon leadership outlawed polygamy in the 1890's.

William Flake had two wives — Lucy Hannah White and Prudence Jane Kartchner. Between them they had 20 children. James Madison Flake was the eldest son of William and Lucy White. James Flake also had two wives but not at the same time. James Flake and Nancy Hall had nine children before she died in 1895. James Flake then married Martha Smith and had 15 more children. By 1969 the descendants of James Flake and his 24 offspring totaled over 1200 and counting. This number does not include any of James Flake's 19 brothers and sisters, many of whom had very large families as well. Large Mormon families are quite common but few were as prolific as the Flake clan.

The Flake family is scattered throughout Mormon communities in Arizona but many still reside in Snowflake. In 1988 the Snowflake Police Chief was Sanford Flake and Flake Willis was on the City Council.

Charles Love Flake was a Justice of the Peace in Snowflake. On December 8, 1892, word came that a New Mexico bank robber named Mason was hiding in a local boarding house. Charles Flake and his older brother James Madison Flake went to arrest the desperado. James grabbed Mason from behind tying up his right hand. But Mason pulled a pistol with his left hand and fired over his shoulder putting a bullet through James Flake's ear. Mason's second shot went into Charles Flake's neck mortally wounding him. Partly blinded by gunpowder, James Flake fired two fatal shots into Mason's head. Charles Flake left four children and a fifth, Charles Jr., was born six months later. The desperado Mason was barely 19 years old and reputedly had already killed seven men.

Snowflake folklore says the tragedy was foretold in a dream. Three months before the tragedy local resident George Gardner warned the Flakes to be careful. Gardner had dreamt "a desperado came and killed Charley and Jim killed him."

Snowflake was incorporated in 1919 and the town promptly outlawed sales of tobacco. Alcohol was already illegal. In 1922 mixed swimming became a local problem out at Silver Creek Dam. A new ordinance allowed males to swim on Tuesday, Thursday and Saturday with females getting the other days of the week. No one swam on Sunday. Suits were recommended out of respect for residents living nearby.

Today the biggest employer is the Stone Forest Industries pulp and paper mill which is 15 miles west of Snowflake. Farming remains a major activity and there are said to be 120,000 pigs in the vicinity. Cattle ranching is also important. A survey in the 1970's found that Snowflake is 70% Mormon. The population in 1989 was about 4,000.

Mormon pioneer James Madison Flake on his LDS mission to Scotland. *Credit — Arizona Historical Society*

AJO

Oldest Mine in Arizona

The remote copper town of Ajo is the oldest known mine site in Arizona. Located in a sparsely populated corner of southwest Arizona, Ajo is surrounded by bleak desert wastelands. Today few visitors go to Ajo except for travelers on their way to Organ Pipe Cactus National Monument or to the beaches at Rocky Point in Mexico.

Long before Europeans arrived here, the Papago Indians obtained paint pigments from the colorful ore deposits. The Papago word "au-auho" means paint and is probably the origin of the town name. In Spanish, Ajo means garlic but sometimes it is used as a swear word. Perhaps early Spanish miners chose the later definition for the hot dry mines. Spanish miners also nicknamed the place Old Bat Hole. Eventually the Spanish mines were abandoned because of Indian raids.

The first Anglo American in Ajo was Tom Childs. In 1847 Childs found a series of open surface cuts and a 60-foot shaft complete with mesquite ladders and rawhide ore buckets. But Childs felt Ajo was too remote to be profitable and moved to Yuma without exploiting his find.

Peter Brady learned of Ajo from Tom Childs and decided to extract the nearly pure native copper found there. From 1854 to 1859 Brady shipped high grade ore to Fort Yuma where it was loaded onto ships and taken to Swansea, Wales for smelting. His second shipload was lost off Patagonia while rounding the treacherous Horn. Brady left Ajo when ore quality decreased and shipping costs ate up the profits. He later married Juanita Mendibles of Altar, Mexico and moved to Tucson where he became Pima County Sheriff.

Various outfits worked the Ajo mines between 1860 and 1884 when Tom Childs returned and took over mining operations. Ajo sputtered along with its low-grade copper ore until 1900 when things really began to change.

A.J. Shotwell was a hot shot mine promoter. He purchased an option from Tom Childs and set about raising money to finance the mine. With John Boddie of St. Louis, Shotwell formed the Cornelia Copper Co. and named it after Boddie's wife. At one point Shotwell tried a "crack pot" smelter idea which claimed to run on gases left over from the smelting process. It was a disastrous failure and Boddie dumped Shotwell as a result. In 1906 Boddie sold out to Col. John C. Greenway, lately of Bisbee.

A new era began with Greenway and the boom times were on. Greenway was familiar with mining low grade copper ores. He formed the New Cornelia Copper Co. and began large scale open pit operations. But one small problem stood in his way. Old Ajo, a bunch of adobe and rock shanties, was situated directly over the proposed open pit. The residents steadfastly refused to move. A mysterious fire swept through Old Ajo and completely destroyed the place. New Cornelia forged ahead.

Greenway found good water supplies at Childs Ranch seven miles north of Ajo and dug deep wells. He built a railroad line to Gila Bend linking up with the Southern Pacific. Greenway also designed New Ajo as a planned community centered around a downtown Spanish-style plaza. In 1921 Greenway sold out to Phelps Dodge which has run Ajo ever since.

One of Phelps Dodge's first actions was to expand water supplies crucial to open pit mining and smelting. They built the giant Ajo Well, sinking two shafts into an aquifer below the dry Rio Cornez. Five massive pumps located 650 feet underground were staffed 24 hours a day and pumped 5,600 gallons a minute to Ajo. The water was 102 degrees and until adequate ventilation men worked in constant 134 degree heat.

"I owe my soul to the company store," was frequently heard on the streets of Ajo. Phelps Dodge, called P.D. by the miners, owned everything in Ajo and used their immense power to drive out any competitors. The only housing in Ajo was owned by Phelps Dodge. In fact almost all buildings and land in Ajo were in the hands of Phelps Dodge. The mining company also ran the utilities and the hospital. And the one store in Ajo was the Phelps Dodge Mercantile which offered everything from food to major appliances. Credit was as easy as showing your P.D. card and signing your name.

Cigarettes were cheap in Ajo. A miner short of cash would sign for 10 cartons of smokes and sell them for 50 cents on the dollar. Of course this just got them further into debt. It's said some miners got no money on payday, just a check stub.

For decades Phelps Dodge had over 1,000 men working in the Ajo mine and smelter. In 1967 there were 1,400 employees. In 1980 there were 1,200. But copper fell on hard times in the 1980's. A bitter labor dispute in 1983 divided the town into scabs and strikers, and bad feelings remain today. In 1984 the mine and smelter closed. By 1986 Phelps Dodge had only 30 employees in caretaker's positions. Ajo population in 1980 was 5,477 but in 1986 it was 2,800. Phelps Dodge put many of its 650 homes on the market. Some retired people moved to Ajo for the cheap houses.

The massive Phelps Dodge Smelter in Ajo about 1930. Note the locomotive and railroad cars for copper bullion. The rail line — Tucson, Cornelia and Gila Bend — linked Ajo with the Southern Pacific system. The open pit mine and smelter closed in 1984. *Credit — Arizona Department of Library & Archives*

GRAND CANYON VILLAGE

Best View in the World

Perched on sheer cliffs, Grand Canyon Village overlooks the most spectacular landscape in the world. Each year some three million people pass through the village while visiting the Grand Canyon. However, most visitors don't realize the townsite was chosen because an ancient Indian trail begins here.

Bright Angel Trail, the "world's most famous footpath," starts at the western edge of Grand Canyon Village. The trail follows Bright Angel fault, a massive geologic crack that bisects the entire canyon. For centuries Havasupai Indians used this natural break in the cliffs to reach their farms at Indian Gardens. Around the turn of the century, Ralph Cameron, a U.S. Senator from Arizona, got private ownership of the trail by filing bogus mine claims along it. In 1928 the National Park Service finally got control of Bright Angel Trail. It is now open to the public at no charge.

Flagstaff stagecoach operator, J. Wilbur Thurber, started the Bright Angel Hotel at the old Indian trailhead in 1896. A mishmash of cabins and tents sprang up around his rambling inn. When the railroad came to Grand Canyon Village, Thurber's stages were put out of business. He sold his hotel to Martin Buggeln, who ran it in association with the railroad for several years.

Buckey O'Neill, a flashy politician from Prescott, provided the impetus for a railroad to Grand Canyon. O'Neill had a copper mine at Anita, 14 miles south of the Canyon. In 1897 he convinced a Chicago firm, Lombard and Goode, to buy the mine and build a railroad to it. Rail tracks reached Anita in 1900 just as copper ore played out. The small railroad went bankrupt and was sold to Santa Fe Railroad. Tracks were extended to Grand Canyon Village and the first Santa Fe passenger train arrived at the Canyon on September 17, 1901.

Grand Canyon Village boomed with the arrival of the railroad. Santa Fe and its affiliate Fred Harvey Co. obtained a 20 acre station grant from the government, and started building a depot, hotel and other facilities. Hotels at other South Rim sites went out of business, and individuals catering to the tourist trade relocated to the railhead. Ramshackle buildings soon clustered around the depot. The first depot was simply a boxcar parked on a side track. The current Santa Fe Railway Station, a rustic log structure, was built in 1909 and is now part of the Grand Canyon Village Historic District.

The majority of early Grand Canyon visitors arrived by train. But about 1930 most visitors started arriving by automobile. Santa Fe finally suspended rail service in 1968. In its final month of operation fewer than 200 people rode the train.

However, a new era began on September 17, 1989 — 88 years to the day after the first train came to the Canyon. On that day a 1901 steam locomotive carried 500 people from Williams to Grand Canyon Village for the first time in 20 years. The Grand Canyon Railway now operates regular service to the Grand Canyon from Williams.

"Capt." John Hance was a former muleskinner who came to Grand Canyon in 1883 on a prospecting trip. He opened Hance Ranch for tourists and built a trail down

President Teddy Roosevelt took a mule ride down Bright Angel Trail in 1911. Behind him on the white mule is "Capt" John Hance, a Grand Canyon guide famous for his tall tales. Also along is the muckraking writer Ida Tarbell and the wealthy Colgate family. *Credit — Kolb Brothers*

Red Canyon. In 1906 Hance sold out and moved to Grand Canyon Village where Bright Angel Lodge gave him free room and board. His job was to entertain guests with his superb storytelling. When President Teddy Roosevelt came to the canyon it was Hance who served as his tour guide.

Hance became famous for his tall tales. Sometimes the Canyon is filled rim to rim with fog while the sky above is perfectly clear. One Hance story claims the clouds were once so thick that he walked over to the North Rim using snowshoes. In another tale Hance claims he dug the canyon all by himself. But one day a child innocently asked, "What did you do with the dirt?" For once in his life Hance was at a loss for words. On his death bed Hance reportedly said to friends, "Where could I have put that dirt?"

In 1919 at age 80 Hance died in Flagstaff at the Coconino County Hospital for the Indigent. He is buried in the Grand Canyon Cemetery just west of the Visitor Center. His gravestone claims "John Hance First Locator on Grand Canyon."

El Tovar Hotel was named for a Spanish explorer who never saw the Grand Canyon. It is the most famous building at Grand Canyon and was the premier establishment of the Fred Harvey chain. Architect Charles Whittlesey created a luxurious "hunting lodge" of native stone and Oregon pine that cost $250,000 to build in 1905. In the 1970's it cost $5,000,000 to remodel the grand hotel. The 100-room hostelry is still famous for comfort, cuisine and VIP visitors. Interior decor features Navajo rugs

In 1908 a trail party departs El Tovar Hotel for a mule ride into the Grand Canyon. The luxurious El Tovar was named for a Spanish explorer who never saw the Grand Canyon. The hotel still provides elegant lodging for contemporary visitors. *Credit — National Park Service*

Grand Canyon photographers par excellence. The Kolb Brothers (Emery and Ellsworth) would do just about anything for a good picture. The Kolbs operated a studio at Grand Canyon Village for some 75 years, and took an estimated 1,500,000 pictures. *Credit — National Park Service*

and Pueblo pottery along with mounted heads of elk, moose, mountain sheep and buffalo.

The Fred Harvey Co. has managed El Tovar and Bright Angel Lodge since 1905. A Park Service contract gave them the main concessions at Grand Canyon Village in 1920. Today Fred Harvey still controls most tourist services from food and lodging to guided tours. Fred Harvey Co. was started in 1876 by an Englishman who soon managed all hotels and restaurants owned by the Santa Fe Railroad. Harvey Houses were famous for luxurious service including fine china, silverware and even fresh flowers. Women employees were called Harvey Girls and wore black dresses with white ruffled trim. This uniform was not changed until 1971. Today Fred Harvey is owned by AMFAC Corporation.

Mary E.J. Colter, architect and designer with Fred Harvey, is the person most responsible for the architectural style of Grand Canyon Village. It's often called NPS Rustic (NPS–National Park Service). Colter's unobtrusive creations always stress compatibility with the natural setting.

Colter, born in 1869, graduated from the California School of Design and later taught high school in St. Paul. Her first building at Grand Canyon was Hopi House. It's modeled after the Hopi village of Oraibi. Colter designed the lower floor as a showroom for Indian art. The upper floors were apartments for Hopi craftsmen.

Lookout Studio, completed in 1914, was another Colter creation. Fred Harvey wanted a photo shop to compete with the energetic Kolb Brothers. Colter designed a rough stone building with an uneven roof line that mirrored the ragged spires in the canyon. Lookout Studio was so "natural" that weeds were planted on the roof in the early years.

Bright Angel Lodge is considered Colter's masterpiece. Completed in 1935, the Lodge is a pioneer-style building of native stone and massive logs. It features a "geologic" fireplace with rockwork that duplicates Grand Canyon strata. Colter carefully incorporated historic buildings into the lodge plan including the Buckey O'Neill Cabin and Red Horse Stage Station.

Mary Colter worked for Fred Harvey nearly 50 years. Hotels and restaurants from Chicago to Los Angeles on the Santa Fe line exhibited her ideas. But her best work was at Grand Canyon. Other buildings include Hermits Rest, Desert WatchTower and Phantom Ranch in the bottom of the canyon. Colter retired in 1948 at age 79. She lived her last years in Santa Fe and passed away in 1958.

Kolb Studio, hanging over the canyon rim, was both home and photo studio for Ellsworth and Emery Kolb for most of this century. The Kolb brothers came to the Grand Canyon in 1902 and Ellsworth was a bellhop for a spell. The brothers bought a photo studio and opened for business at the Bright Angel Trailhead. Their first darkroom was an abandoned mine with a canvas sheet door.

The enterprising Kolb brothers made the first motion pictures of a Colorado River boat trip in 1912. This made them nationally famous. They opened a showroom at their Grand Canyon studio in 1915 and eventually gave over 50,000 showings of the film. It's also estimated they took some 1,500,000 photos of canyon tourists. The precarious studio reached its present size in 1926. The building annoyed many naturalists who wanted it removed. But the Kolbs had powerful friends in government and their unique place was preserved.

Ellsworth Kolb died in 1960. That same year Emery's wife Blanche also died. Emery Kolb, who stood about five feet tall, took his last Colorado River boat trip in 1974 at age 93. He died two years later. After his death a mysterious skeleton was found in the Kolb brothers boat which hung from the studio ceiling for many years.

The biggest problem at Grand Canyon Village has always been water. In the early years all water was brought in on railroad tank cars. In 1931 a six-inch pipeline was constructed from Indian Gardens to the South Rim. Another pipeline was built in 1966 which transports water all the way across the canyon from Roaring Springs below the North Rim.

Grand Canyon National Park was set up in 1919 and the Park Service has been the Village city government ever since. Many early buildings have been set aside as a Historic District. These include El Tovar, Hopi House, Kolb Studio, Lookout Studio and the mule barns which were built in 1907 and are still in use today.

Grand Canyon Village is a fully functioning town with bank, post office, hospital, garage and gas station, barber and beauty shops, laundry, churches, pet kennels, and even Rotary and Lions clubs.

Lookout Studio at Grand Canyon was designed by Mary Colter for the Fred Harvey Co. in 1914. The flat roof was added later. The roof of Colter's original building was planted with weeds to make it look more natural. *Credit — Author*

Hopi House at Grand Canyon Village was designed by Mary Colter and inspired by the Hopi village of Oraibi. Hopi House opened New Years Day, 1905 and continues to sell Indian arts and crafts to this day. *Credit — Santa Fe Railway*

This is Front Street (now Santa Fe Ave.) in Flagstaff in 1894. Concrete sidewalks are beginning to replace wooden boardwalks. The flat cars belong to the Atlantic and Pacific Railroad which later became the Santa Fe Railroad. *Credit — Author's collection*

FLAGSTAFF

Beside the Sleeping Volcano

Nicknamed Flag, this mountain town is the trading, government and education center for northern Arizona. Flagstaff started as a railroad town on the Atlantic and Pacific (now Santa Fe) line back in 1881. Today it has a population over 40,000. Flagstaff is county seat for Coconino, the second largest county in the U.S. and larger than Massachusetts and Vermont combined.

Flagstaff sits at the base of an ancient volcano, San Francisco Peaks. The mountain rises 12,670 feet and is Arizona's highest point. The Peaks are sacred to Indians in the region. They are home to the Hopi Kachinas or "ancestor gods." The Peaks are also one of four sacred mountains of the Navajo.

An old myth said San Francisco Peaks were named because you could see the California city from the top. Not true. From the Peaks one can see 200 miles but San Francisco is over 700 miles away. San Francisco Peaks were named by Spanish missionaries at Hopiland in 1629.

The origin of Flagstaff's unique name has been debated by various historians. One story says a Boston group, the Arizona Colonization Co., stripped a lone pine and raised the American flag here on July 4, 1876. These colonists found the area too remote and moved to more civilized locales.

Another story has Lt. Beale and his survey party creating the first flagpole. Beale established a wagon road across northern Arizona in 1859. But Beale was not the first surveyor to travel this route. Capt. Sitgreaves in 1851 and Lt. Whipple in 1854 preceded Beale, and both men were guided by Antoine Leroux. From his home in Taos, New Mexico, Leroux often traveled this route in the 1830's and 1840's to get to California.

Perhaps the most obscure story is actually the correct one. According to one source, the first flagstaff was a thick canvas sheet tied atop a pine tree stripped of its branches. This flagstaff was erected to mark Antelope Spring, which was later called Flagstaff Spring and later still Old Town Spring. Finding water was a life and death matter to early travelers in dry country. Due to porous volcanic soils, there are no dependable streams for miles around Flagstaff. The flag at Antelope Spring was a signal alerting cross country travelers to the hard-to-find water source. This spring was at the base of Mars Hill near downtown Flagstaff.

It is certain, however, that there was more than one flagstaff at Flagstaff. Early pioneers report at least two huge pine tree flagstaffs. One was at Old Town Flagstaff (at Flagstaff Spring) and another was located one mile east near the railroad depot. Neither of these flagstaffs survived past 1900.

Flagstaff sprang up boom town fashion shortly before the railroad arrived. The Atlantic and Pacific Railroad got a U.S. charter to build along the 34th parallel route back in 1866. No work was done until 1870. As incentive, the government gave the railroad 40 square miles of adjoining land (in alternate sections) for every mile of track they laid. Much of this land was sold to huge cattle companies like the Hashknife Ranch.

On August 1, 1882 the Atlantic and Pacific Railroad arrived at Flagstaff. The railroad had entered Arizona in 1880. It finally completed the line across Arizona in 1883 when it bridged the Colorado River at Needles.

The Atlantic and Pacific, later to become the Santa Fe, was an economic bonanza to northern Arizona. Lumber and livestock producers used the Flagstaff depot to get quick access to remote markets. Later tourists used the railroad to visit Grand Canyon and other attractions.

Before the railroad arrived, the town was clustered around Flagstaff Spring. The entire business district moved one mile east when the railroad depot was built at that location. Flagstaff's main street, Santa Fe Avenue, still runs parallel to the railroad.

The first large scale industrial company in Arizona was the Ayer Sawmill at Flagstaff. E.E. Ayer of Chicago spent $150,000 in 1882 to ship and set up a complete sawmill. He hired oxen teams to haul the sawmill equipment from the railroad construction terminal at Winslow. This allowed Ayer to have the sawmill in full operation when the railroad arrived at Flagstaff.

The Ayer Sawmill employed 250 men and had a capacity of 100,000 board feet a day. It produced a variety of wood products and had shingle, lath and planing mills. A company village grew up at the sawmill and was named Milton for the famous English poet. A huge boarding house at Milton housed 150 men. Lumber from the Ayer Sawmill was exported to California, New Mexico and even into Mexico.

Flagstaff sits at the northern end of the world's largest Ponderosa pine forest. This vast timberland extends for 200 miles into New Mexico and is about 50 miles wide. From the railroad Ayer obtained an option in 87 square miles of forest to the south and west of Flagstaff. This guaranteed a steady supply of trees for his sawmill.

Ayer sold his sawmill to D.M. Riordan in 1887. Riordan changed the name to Arizona Lumber and Timber. Riordan was a former Navajo Indian Agent who joined the Ayer Sawmill as a manager. Two other Riordan brothers, Timothy and Michael, helped run the sawmill.

D.M. Riordan was a partner in the Mineral Belt Railroad which was to run from Flagstaff to Globe. A 3,100-foot tunnel was proposed to cut through the rugged Mogollon Rim but only 200 feet was ever completed. This tunnel, located at the headwaters of the East Verde River, is now a popular hike. Only 70 miles of track were laid and Riordan made good use of this portion to haul logs to his sawmill.

The Riordans, Timothy and Michael, married two sisters, Caroline and Elizabeth Metz of Ohio. The Metz sisters were first cousins of the famous Babbitt family. The Riordans built twin mansions side by side in south Flagstaff so the sisters could be next-door neighbors. Their houses are now a State Park.

John Young, son of Mormon leader Brigham Young, founded the first big cattle company in the Flagstaff area. The Moroni Cattle Co., named for a Mormon angel, was started in 1881 in Fort Valley. Young, with a dozen other Mormon families, built Fort Moroni using double-length railroad ties set into the ground. This served as the headquarters for the ranch. However Young, who had several wives, fled Arizona soon afterward fearing arrest for polygamy.

In 1885 the Moroni Cattle Co. became the Arizona Cattle Co. which was better known as the A-1. It's said the A-1 outfit had the finest range in the state. It ran from the Grand Canyon to Lake Mary and from Ash Fork to the Little Colorado River ... or 400 square miles of grazing lands. The A-1 ran some 16,000 head of cattle on this property. The A-1 was controlled by New York money men. Old Fort Moroni became Fort Rickerson, named for Charles Rickerson of New York, who was director of the Arizona Cattle Co.

At one time sheep were even more important to Flagstaff than cattle. It is estimated there were 150,000 sheep around Flagstaff in the late 1880's. Many were owned by the Daggs Brothers, who had been in the area since 1875. With headquarters in Flagstaff, the Daggs Brothers owned some 50,000 sheep. But it is said that the largest sheep herd was owned by Walter Hill who had a ranch west of Flagstaff. Hart Prairie, Elden Mountain and Ashurst Lake are well known area landmarks that were named for prominent local sheepmen.

The Daggs Brothers were involved in the famous Pleasant Valley War which took place in the Tonto Basin southeast of Flagstaff. One faction in the dispute, the Tewksburys, got sheep "on share" from the Daggs Brothers. The Grahams, the other faction, were cattlemen who objected to forage lost to the ravenous sheep. Many were killed on both sides but it is said the sheepmen "won" the war. The Graham family was virtually wiped out.

The Babbitts are Flagstaff's premier family. They came from Cincinnati, Ohio, where the family owned a grocery store. The Babbitt's moved west seeking opportunity and soon became the dominant economic force in northern Arizona.

There were five original Babbitt brothers ... David, George, William, Charles (CJ), and Edward. In Ohio they lived across the street from Gerald Verkamp and his nine kids. David was to marry Emma Verkamp, CJ wed Mary Verkamp, and Edward married Matilda Verkamp. Eventually all five brothers moved to Flagstaff.

The first Babbitt brother arrived in Flagstaff in 1886 with a $20,000 draft to purchase a cattle ranch. David Babbitt bought 864 head and started the CO Bar Ranch (CO = Cincinnati, Ohio). Their first cabin was where Lake Mary is now. The Babbitt's expanded into one of the largest ranching outfits in the U.S. They later bought the

The Riordan Mansion in south Flagstaff is now a State Park. Lumber barons, Timothy and Michael Riordan, married two sisters, Caroline and Elizabeth Metz. Together the two families shared separate wings of this spacious mansion. *Credit — Author*

huge A-1 Ranch and the famous Hashknife Ranch. Other big Babbitt ranches were Cataract Livestock near Grand Canyon, and Hart Cattle at Winslow. In 1915 the Babbitt's sold their cattle crop for $1,500,000 which set a record for many years.

Cattle was just one feature of the Babbitt empire. In 1888 Babbitt Hardware opened and the next year Babbitt Trading Co. was formed. In 1891 the Babbitts bought the first of many Trading Posts they owned on the Hopi and Navajo reservations. Babbitt's general stores were later found in many northern Arizona towns including Williams, Holbrook, Winslow, Kingman and Page. The Babbitts also owned sheep ranches, hotels, an auto dealership, assorted real estate, a slaughter house and meat packing plant, mortuary, livery stable, ice plant, garage, bank, a fox farm and even an opera house.

Bruce Babbitt, Arizona Governor from 1978 to 1986, is the most famous son of the Babbitt family. Bruce's father Paul was son of Charles (CJ) Babbitt. Bruce was born and raised in Los Angeles where his mother was a violinist with LA Philharmonic. His father later moved back to Flagstaff when family business required his presence.

Bruce Babbitt was educated at Notre Dame and Harvard. He was elected Arizona Attorney General in 1974. When Gov. Wesley Bolin died unexpectedly on March 4, 1978, Bruce Babbitt became Governor. In 1979 Bruce became the youngest elected Governor of Arizona at age 40. In 1988 he ran for president in the Democratic primary but finished back in the pack.

The Babbitt family is still prominent in Flagstaff but their dominance is greatly reduced. One Babbitt recently served as Flagstaff mayor. However, the family no longer owns the Babbitt store chain.

Lowell Observatory sits on Mars Hill above downtown Flagstaff. It is the site of many important astronomical discoveries. It was founded by Percival Lowell, scion of the wealthy Boston textile family, back in 1894. Percival's brother Abbott was president of Harvard, and his sister Amy was a renown poet.

Mars was Lowell's specialty and he designed his observatory to study the Red Planet. Lowell wrote a book, "Mars and Its Canals," based on his work in Flagstaff. Mars is still an important area of study at Lowell but other discoveries have become better known.

The discovery of Planet X was predicted by Percival Lowell in 1916, the same year he died. In 1930 Lowell astronomer Clyde Tombaugh found Planet X on photo plates taken by the Observatorie's 13-inch telescope. The ninth planet was later renamed Pluto.

Another early achievement was Dr. Vesto Slipher's work at Lowell. Slipher found the "red shift" in galaxies which led to the theory of an expanding universe.

Lowell Observatory has made Flagstaff an important extraterrestrial research center. The Naval Observatory came to Flagstaff in 1955 partly because Lowell was located nearby. In 1965 NASA built the Planetary Research Center with fire-proof vaults at Lowell Observatory. Later Apollo astronauts trained near Flagstaff at Meteor Crater and other locations preparing for their moon landing.

Lowell Observatory now operates several telescopes in and around Flagstaff. Largest is a 72-inch Perkins Reflector installed on a mountain top about 10 miles south of town back in 1961. Next largest is a 41-inch scope dating from 1909. There are also several 20-inch reflectors and refractors. An instrument shop at Lowell builds special equipment needed for these telescopes.

The tomb of Percival Lowell at his Observatory. Lowell predicted the discovery of Pluto and wrote a book, "Mars and Its Canals." Lowell Observatory is a world famous astronomical facility with many telescopes located on mountains around Flagstaff. *Credit — Author*

Lowell chose Flagstaff for his Observatory because of the clear air caused by the high altitude. But today some 12,000 wood burning fireplaces often cause serious visible air pollution.

Lowell Observatory is open to the public. The main attraction is the historic 24-inch Clark telescope that Lowell used for his work on Mars. Lowell's Tomb with its unusual purple glass dome is also worth viewing.

Northern Arizona University (NAU) is one of three universities in Arizona but it is the only one to begin as a reform school. In 1893 money was approved for a reform school at Flagstaff. Buildings were constructed but local citizens opposed the reform school and it never opened. In 1899 Northern Arizona Normal School set up class-rooms in the unused buildings. In 1901 a total of four women were graduated in the first class. In 1925 the school became Arizona State Teachers College offering four-year degrees. Today NAU is a major institution best known for its School of Forestry.

The Flagstaff Festival of the Arts began in 1965 and has now become an annual event each summer. The Festival attracts well-known artists for classical music, dance and theatre performances.

The All-Indian Pow Wow began in Flagstaff back in 1930. The Pow Wow brought Indians from across the nation to Flag and grew to massive proportions in the early 1970's. In 1972 ten militant Indians were arrested for disrupting the Pow Wow and this marked the beginning of the end. Other problems included large numbers of Indians camping in the city park. In 1973 the Pow Wow was canceled. It was revived in 1975 but the city decided it was too great a burden and it was canceled again.

Chiricahua Apache chieftain Geronimo (on horse next to the child) and Nachez (with hat) appear in this famous photograph by C.S. Fly at the time of their surrender in 1886. Afterwards all Chiricahua Apaches, including U.S. Army Scouts and Indians who remained on the reservation, were banished from their homeland and imprisoned in Florida and Oklahoma.

FORT HUACHUCA – SIERRA VISTA

A Classic "Main Gate" Town

Sierra Vista, Spanish for "mountain view," is one of the newest and fastest growing cities in Arizona. It's a "main gate" town and exists solely to supply civilian services to the sprawling U.S. Army base at Fort Huachuca. Today Fort Huachuca is headquarters for Army Electronic Communications and site of the Army Intelligence Center. It's also the largest single employer in all southern Arizona with nearly 12,000 jobs.

Fort Huachuca was established in 1877 by Capt. Samuel Marmaduke Whitside to protect settlers from Apache and Mexican attacks. Located at 4,600 feet on the east slope of the Huachuca Mountains, the fort commands a panoramic view of the San Pedro River valley. Huachuca is a Sobaipuri Indian word that means "place of thunder, wind and rain."

Fort Huachuca is the only "Indian Wars" fort to remain an active military base. Almost all original buildings are still standing and in day-to-day use. The oldest structure is the 1880 Post Hospital, now a private residence for Army brass. Four barracks buildings built in 1884 are now used for offices. A row of two-story adobe homes are still used as officers quarters. This historical area is clustered around the old parade grounds and is open to the public. The Fort Huachuca Historical Museum and Annex provide numerous displays on local military history.

Geronimo, the famous Apache war chief, was pursued by Fort Huachuca troops during his fourth and final campaign to escape reservation life. The chase led all over southern Arizona and northern Mexico. For 15 months Geronimo eluded 6,000 U.S. soldiers, 500 Indian scouts, various vigilante groups, and numerous Mexican troops. Geronimo had 35 men, eight boys and 101 women and children. In this campaign the Apaches killed 75 American civilians, 12 White Mountain Apaches, eight soldiers and a large but unknown number of Mexican citizens. The Apaches lost six men (two of whom were on a peace mission) as well as two women and an infant.

Constant harassment from Fort Huachuca soldiers finally forced Geronimo to surrender at Skeleton Canyon on September 3, 1886. When he gave up Geronimo was wearing the shirt of Capt. Hatfield, D Troop, 4th Cavalry, Fort Huachuca. Hatfield lost his horse and possessions in an early skirmish with the Apaches. Geronimo and his band were first sent to Florida and then later confined in Oklahoma until the death of the old chief.

Geronimo's surrender ended Arizona's Indian Wars with one notable exception. The Apache Kid, a former Indian Army Scout, was convicted of assault on a superior officer and sentenced to Yuma Territorial Prison in 1889. However, the Apache Kid and seven other Apaches escaped en route to prison by killing the sheriff and deputy transporting them. All the Apaches except the Kid were soon killed or captured. For 20 years reports linked the Apache Kid to numerous killings and kidnappings. Fort Huachuca sent troops into the field many times but the elusive Kid was never captured. And the $5,000 reward on his head was never claimed.

Fort Huachuca became home base for the Army's Indian Scouts when Fort Apache was closed in 1922. At one time 1,000 Indians were employed as scouts and attached to forts throughout Arizona. But after Geronimo's surrender only 150 were retained. At Fort Huachuca the Scouts lived with their families in traditional wickiups and chose not to live in the "white man's" houses the Army provided. There were no new enlistments after World War I and the last Indian Scout was deactivated in 1947.

Nicknames were standard since few white men could pronounce Apache names. Eskehnedestah was called Sgt. Chicken after his favorite food. Other Fort Huachuca Scouts were Sgt. Deadshot, Sgt. Peaches, Sgt. Big Chow, Sgt. Charlie Bones and Cpl. Dandy Jim. The Indian Scouts were an essential feature of U.S. Army presence in Territorial Arizona and credited with the success of the Indian Campaigns.

Buffalo Soldiers are another little known facet of Fort Huachuca and Arizona history. The all-black Army units were called Buffalo soldiers because Indians noted their hair resembled the shaggy mane of the American bison. Every all-black U.S. Army unit was stationed at Fort Huachuca at one time or another. They were the 9th and 10th Cavalry, the 24th and 25th Infantry, and in World War II, the 92nd and 93rd Infantry Divisions. They were usually commanded by white officers but some whites refused to accept these assignments. One officer who refused duty with the Buffalo Soldiers was General George Custer. One black officer who served at Fort Huachuca was the first black graduate of West Point, Lt. Henry Flipper.

During World War II the 92nd Infantry or the Buffalo Division trained at Fort Huachuca before shipping out for duty in Italy. Many famous black entertainers came to the local USO Club including Pearl Bailey, Satchmo, and Lena Horne, who was elected Sweetheart of the 92nd. President Truman desegregated the Army before the Korean War. Sierra Vista retains a large black population to this day.

This is Company C, 6th Cavalry dressed out in their finest uniforms for a muster at Fort Huachuca about 1883. Note the large shade trees and enlisted men's barracks in the background. *Credit — Arizona Historical Society*

Twenty miles north of Mexico, Fort Huachuca owes its long life to its location near the volatile international border. The Fort was very active during the Mexican Revolution (1910-1920). Many battles between Mexican Revolutionists and Federales took place on the Arizona border including Nogales, Naco and Agua Prieta. Troops from Fort Huachuca were stationed along the border to keep hostilities from crossing the line. The most violent clash involving Fort Huachuca troops occurred at Nogales in 1913 when a number of Mexicans were killed.

Pancho Villa raided Columbus, New Mexico in 1916 and General Black Jack Pershing was sent into Mexico after him. The Punitive Expedition included the 10th Cavalry (Buffalo Soldiers) from Fort Huachuca who were sent into Chihuahua. The slogan "Villa Dead or Alive' gave way several months later to "almost caught Villa." U.S. troops left Mexico without ever catching up with Pancho Villa and his Revolutionary Army.

A famous resident of Fort Huachuca in 1890 was Fiorella LaGuardia, later Mayor of New York City from 1934 to 1945. His father Achille LaGuardia was an enlisted man attached to the Army Band. Fiorella became "socially aware" when he saw Army units put down the 1894 Pullman Railroad Strike and "defend only employers not workers." He was also "disgusted" with the treatment of Indians he saw in Arizona. He credits these early experiences with "firing up" his liberal political career.

During World War II as many as 25,000 troops were stationed at Fort Huachuca for training. Many new barracks and other buildings were built. But in 1947 it was temporarily deactivated and "given" to the Arizona Game and Fish Department. Ironically Game and Fish established a buffalo herd at the fort which once numbered some 450 animals. However, the Army soon wanted the fort back. In 1954 Fort Huachuca was reopened to become the Army's space age center.

The U.S. Army Electronic Proving Ground was first to set up headquarters at Fort Huachuca. They tested unmanned drone aircraft for photo reconnaissance, taking advantage of the good weather conditions at the fort. In 1966 the 11th Signal Group, which installs and maintains the worldwide Army communications system, moved to Fort Huachuca. The next year saw the arrival of the Army Communications Command from Washington, D.C. In 1971 the Army Intelligence Center and School relocated here from Maryland. Today Fort Huachuca is one of the most important Army bases in the world. It's responsible for many aspects of Army Communications, Intelligence and Electronic Warfare. It's a far cry from the 1880's when long distance messages were sent by Army heliograph (sunlight reflected on mirrors).

Sierra Vista was incorporated with a population of 1,700 in 1955. But a "main gate" town has always existed just east of the fort. The first community was called Garden Creek. The name changed to Buena about 1915. In 1937 it was called Fry for a local homesteader. Fort Huachuca itself was annexed by Sierra Vista in 1971 and the population soared to 15,000. Today Sierra Vista has some 30,000 residents, which is much larger than the county seat at Bisbee.

Retirees make up 25% of Sierra Vista's population but only 6% of the people are over 60 years of age. Most of these retirees are from the military which allows servicemen to retire after 20 years of active duty.

A modern historical footnote concerns the $18,000,000 "aerostat" balloon stationed at Fort Huachuca by the U.S. Customs Service. The nine-ton radar balloon is attached to the ground with two miles of cable. It was unveiled in 1987 by Arizona Senator Dennis DeConcini. It is supposed to catch low flying drug smuggling aircraft but after one year of operation it was batting zero. Many Sierra Vista citizens oppose the balloon and fear it may crash into their homes. They have dubbed the balloon "DeConcini's Delight."

Artillery piece on the parade ground in front of the Fort Huachuca Historical Museum. Visitors are welcome but must obtain a "pass" at the main gate. *Credit — Author*

CLIFTON

A Tough Copper Town in Apache County

Clifton, known for bitter and often violent labor disputes, is the copper mining center of eastern Arizona. The rambling town of 4,000 people is located in narrow canyons beside the flood-prone San Francisco River. Clifton is also county seat for Greenlee County, a thin strip of land sandwiched between the Apache Reservations and New Mexico wilderness areas.

One tale says the town was named for Henry Clifton who led a prospecting group through here in 1864. But Clifton was chased out by Apaches long before the town began. The more popular version says Charlie Shannon observed the steep hillsides above the growing smelter town and called the place Cliff Town. This was later shortened to Clifton.

Bob and Jim Metcalfe, two brothers employed as Army scouts, passed through the area in 1870 and noted the rich ore deposits. Two years later they returned and staked claims to the Longfellow and Metcalfe mines. Soon afterwards the Metcalfe brothers sold the Longfellow Mine to two merchants from New Mexico, the brothers Henry and Charles Lesinsky.

The Lesinsky's built a crude adobe-walled smelter and hired Mexican workers from Juarez to run it. They shipped copper ingots to Kansas City in wagons pulled by oxen. On the return trip, the Lesinsky wagons were loaded with supplies for their general stores.

The Longfellow Mine was five miles from Clifton and about 2500 feet higher. To get ore to the smelter in Clifton, mules would pull empty ore cars up to the mine. Then, using gravity, the mules would ride back down with the fully-laden ore cars.

The Lesinsky brothers built the first railroad in Arizona when they replaced mules with steam power in 1878. A mini-locomotive, dubbed the Little Emma, was hauled 700 miles overland from the rail terminal in La Junta, Colorado. For many years Little Emma was operated by engineer Henry "Dad" Arbuckle. Today Little Emma is at the Arizona Museum in Phoenix.

Frank Underwood of Kansas City bought out the Lesinsky's in 1882. He paid $1,500,000 for all their Clifton property including mines, smelter, stores and rolling stock. Within months Underwood turned around and sold all of it for $2,000,000 to Scottish investors. Thus was born the Arizona Copper Company Ltd., with headquarters in Edinburgh, Scotland. Arizona Copper Company was to be the prime mover in Clifton for the next 40 years.

Arizona Copper brought in managers and foremen from Scotland to run the operation. Some of their descendants still live in the area. As a result, Clifton is the only town in Arizona to field cricket and rugby teams.

Mining operations expanded quickly when Arizona Copper came to Clifton. The company built a 71-mile railroad, the Arizona and New Mexico, to link up with the Southern Pacific line at Lordsburg, New Mexico. They also built a sawmill, an electric plant, an ice plant and various other facilities.

The Arizona Copper smelter was located in downtown Clifton at the junction of Chase Creek and the San Francisco River. It was the same site as the Lesinsky

In 1907 Clifton was a grimy industrial city with several thousand residents. Across the flood prone San Francisco River is the Arizona Copper Co. smelter which fills the mouth of Chase Creek. Note the smoke rising from the hill just right of the smelter. A tunnel was drilled into this hill to direct smelter smoke away from the polluted city. This led some residents to joke that Clifton was built beside an active volcano. *Credit — Arizona Historical Society*

smelter and chosen because large quantities of water were needed. Arizona Copper enlarged the smelter but pollution soon became a major problem. Downstream farmers had to sue Arizona Copper to make them reduce toxic wastes dumped into the river.

Clifton residents were also plagued with thick clouds of foul air that spewed from the smelter. To reduce air pollution, a tunnel was cut into a nearby hill and smoke escaped out a hole on top. This gave rise to tall tales about how Clifton was built on top of an active volcano.

About 1890 the high grade copper ore gave out and Arizona Copper suffered setbacks. Shares of Arizona Copper were only worth 75¢ in 1892. But James Colquhoun, a Scot who ran the smelter, developed a method using sulfuric acid that made low grade copper ore profitable. Colquhoun was made General Manager and the company was in the black again. In 1907 shares of Arizona Copper were selling for $80.00 each.

Serious labor problems began in 1903. The Territorial Legislature passed a law that reduced the miners legal work day from 10 hours to eight hours. Copper companies in Clifton and nearby Morenci promptly reduced wages. Angry miners walked out and started a bitter strike. Copper company executives claimed that foreign-born agitators were planning to blow up mine property and loot company stores. As a result the famous Arizona Rangers, the first statewide police organization, was dispatched to keep order. Later Arizona National Guard troops were sent in. The miners did not have an effective union and the strike failed.

During World War I copper prices reached an all-time high. But in Clifton wage rates were far behind other Arizona mine towns. One reason for low wages was the large number of Mexican workers in the district. This was not true in other mining towns at the time. To remedy the problem, workers called in the Western Federation of Miners. Two WFM organizers, Guy Miller and a half-breed Mexican named Tribolet, arrived in August 1915. On September 11, 1915 a general strike was called and 5,000 miners joined it.

Governor George Hunt, from the mine town of Globe, was sympathetic to the strikers. He came to Clifton on September 28 and addressed a rally of miners. Pro copper company newspapers attacked Hunt viciously. One paper said, "He caused the strikers to spit in the face of good citizens by telling them that they were as good as anyone."

On October 2, 1915 the copper company managers left town on a secret train and set up headquarters in El Paso. Striking miners ran strike breakers out of town. They were relocated in a "tent city" in nearby Duncan. Mine executives lobbied for federal troops which had been used to break other recent strikes. Governor Hunt beat them to the punch and ordered in 450 Arizona National Guard troops who adopted a neutral stance.

Finally on January 31, 1916 the strike was settled. Wages were raised and grievance committees were established. Laborers were now to be paid $2.50 a day, miners made $3.41 a day, and machinists got $5.31 a day. But the peace was short-lived. In July 1917 another strike broke out. It was ended when President Wilson sent a commission to resolve the conflict in November. It would not be the last outbreak.

Arizona Copper Co. suffered because the labor disputes came when copper prices were at their height. To make matters worse, copper prices collapsed in 1920.

In 1921 Arizona Copper sold their eight mines including the Longfellow, Coronado, and Metcalfe to Phelps Dodge, who already owned the nearby Morenci mines. Phelps Dodge now had total control of the district. But the shrewd Scottish investors made money again. Part of the deal was 50,000 shares of Phelps Dodge stock. The Scots sold these shares early in 1929 for $300 each. Three years later Phelps Dodge stock sold for only $7 a share.

Copper prices fell to 5¢ a pound in 1932 and all Clifton area mines closed. The population of Clifton fell to 1,500, down from 5,000 or more. In 1937 copper rose to 13¢ a pound and Phelps Dodge prepared to reopen the Morenci mine. But the company had not paid its taxes, over $1,000,000. The state ordered seizure of Phelps Dodge property but the company finally paid up. Clifton got a much needed $100,000 from the delinquent taxes.

Clifton's latest labor problems began in July 1983 when Phelps Dodge cut wages and benefits to its workers. Thirteen unions walked off the job. A court order limited the number of pickets at Phelps Dodge plants. The Arizona Highway Department built a berm along roads leading to the mines to prevent parking anywhere near Phelps Dodge property. Greenlee County Supervisors imposed a 9 p.m. to 6 a.m. curfew. The Clifton City Council, which was pro-strike, refused to honor the curfew and tried to help the strikes but could do little.

"It's controlled civil war," said a Clifton professional. Violence between strikers and scabs (strikebreakers) became common. Governor Bruce Babbitt ordered Arizona Department of Public Safety (DPS) officers to Clifton to keep order. However, the strikers claimed the State Police acted like Phelps Dodge guards and only protected strikebreakers.

On June 30, 1984 a rally drew 1,000 people to Clifton to mark the one-year anniversary of the strike. After the rally DPS Chief Ralph Milstead led 130 officers through Clifton firing rubber bullets at rock-throwing strikers. DPS officers fired tear gas into the Clifton Liquor Store and arrested anyone who came out. One of those tear-gassed and arrested was the store owner who was also nine months pregnant. A lawsuit was filed against DPS and a court found the police had used unnecessary force. However, the strike eventually failed.

The hero of the 1983/1984 strike was Dr. Jorge O'Leary, a Mexican born and educated physician. O'Leary was fired from Phelps Dodge Hospital after he criticized the company and its health care system. Dr. O'Leary promptly opened a Peoples Clinic in Clifton and treated strikers and their families for free. Alice Miller, owner of Clifton Liquors, named her newborn son Jorge, for Dr. O'Leary's efforts.

Floods have been a constant threat to Clifton. One of the first recorded floods was in 1891. The raging waters destroyed the Wells Fargo office and carried the heavy safe into the river. The safe was never found and thousands of dollars in valuables were lost.

In 1903 heavy rain caused the Arizona Copper Co. concentrator dam to fail. A wall of water roared down Chase Creek and into the San Francisco River. Many Mexican citizens lost their lives. Another victim was a Chinese merchant who went back into his store to get his savings. The body of the Chinese man was later recovered but his bag of gold worth $3,000 was never found.

Three years later 18 people lost their lives when a flood swept through Clifton on December 4, 1906. It's said all the Mexican adobe houses were washed away or melted at their foundations. All but one house — which became known as La Arca de Noe or Noah's Ark.

Another flood occurred in 1972 when 150 houses, 50 trailers, and numerous cars were heavily damaged. One of the latest floods happened in October 1983 after eight inches of rain fell in the area. The San Francisco River crested at six feet over the bridges. Several million dollars in damage was reported with 50 homes destroyed and 230 homes damaged. No one was killed, however.

A recent federal government study said there was no way to protect Clifton from floods. The report recommended moving the entire town to "tabletop" land three miles southeast. Clifton residents balked at the suggestion. They went back to repairing flood walls which are a prominent feature of the town landscape. However, a number of the most dangerous residential areas have been abandoned.

A Mexican woman, known as Santa Teresa, was Clifton's most famous "religious" leader. Some said she was a Yaqui priestess and a dangerous heretic. Others said she had divine healing powers, Teresa Urrea was born in 1872 in Sinaloa, Mexico. At age 16 she went into a three-month-long trance, and when she awoke it's said her touch could heal the sick. She was forced to flee Mexico because of pressure from the Catholic Church. She settled in Clifton in 1897.

After a disastrous first marriage, Teresa Urrea later married John Vanoder and had two daughters. She built a large two-story "hospital" in Clifton and ministered to the sick for several years. But in 1906 she died of tuberculosis. In her short life Teresa Urrea earned the love of many who declared her to be Arizona's only Saint.

Another colorful but definitely unscrupulous Clifton character was Rufus Nephew, better known as Climax Jim. It's said he was a petty crook who did his misdeeds with a flair. His most famous caper was the Case of the Disappearing Check. In 1906 Climax Jim tried to buy a hat with a forged check. At his trial this check was placed upon the lawyers' table. Problem was that Climax Jim was sitting at the table too. Before it could be entered as evidence, the check mysteriously vanished. Eaten by Climax Jim said the smart money. Case dismissed.

Climax Jim's other exploits included safe cracking and cattle rustling. But he died young. They say he was digging a well and accidentally dropped a bottle of nitroglycerin.

Clifton Cliff Jail, the first town jail, is now a tourist attraction. It was built about 1878 by Margarite Varela. The Lesinsky brothers paid Varela to blast the jail out of solid rock and lay stone blocks across the opening. His work finished, Margarite spent his profits on mescal, an alcoholic cactus drink popular in Mexico. Varela was arrested that same night for shooting up Hovey's Dance Hall. Thus he became the jail's first occupant as well as its builder.

This is Phoenix founder Jack Swilling with his adopted Apache son Gavilan. Swilling organized the first irrigation ditch company in Phoenix. Known to have killed several men, Swilling was infamous as a mean drunk. It got him in trouble late in life. Swilling died in the Yuma Territorial Prison accused of stagecoach robbery. *Credit — Author's collection*

PHOENIX

A Sprawling Sunbelt Metropolis

Phoenix, with nearly 1,000,000 residents, has grown from a sleepy farm town into the largest city in the Southwest. Like its namesake, this sprawling Sunbelt metropolis arose from the ashes of an ancient Indian civilization. It all began back in 1867 when a roughneck Indian fighter talked some friends into helping him dig a ditch.

The founder of Phoenix was Jack Swilling, a controversial hot-tempered redhead with shoulder-length hair. He came to Arizona about 1858 from South Carolina. Swilling was an infamous fighter and drinker. These traits endeared him to fellow fortune hunters and other hellraisers but it also created bitter enemies. He was known to have killed several white men. As Captain of the Gila Rangers, an Apache-hunting vigilante group, Swilling no doubt killed many Indians as well. But lasting fame came from opening up the vast agricultural lands of the Valley of the Sun.

Jack Swilling was not the first settler in the Salt River Valley. John Y.T. Smith set up a "hay camp" along the Salt River to harvest native grasses in 1865. Smith sold this fodder for cavalry horses to Fort McDowell, 30 miles east of Phoenix.

Swilling was a mail contractor whose travels took him through the Salt River Valley in 1866. He observed the many Indian ruins in the area. Some very large ruins were miles from the river. Swilling realized the long parallel mounds leading from the river to the ruins were overgrown remnants of an extensive canal system.

The canals were built by the Hohokam. The name Hohokam comes from the Pima Indians and means "vanished people" or "people who came before." Living in 30 scattered villages, the industrious Hohokam built nearly 300 miles of irrigation canals and farmed some 40,000 acres in the Phoenix area alone.

For some mysterious reason the Hohokam abandoned their farms about 1400 A.D. Some theorists say the Apache drove them out. Others say a revolution overthrew the priest class and the social organization maintaining the canal system collapsed.

Another possibility is the Hohokam success lead to their downfall. The huge canal system may have raised the ground water table so high that Hohokam fields became waterlogged. This happened in the early 1900's but mechanical pumps quickly lowered the water table again. At any rate the Hohokam civilization had "vanished" several hundred years before Swilling arrived on the scene.

In late 1867 Jack Swilling organized the Swilling Ditch Company with two dozen other men including Henry Wickenburg and Darrell Duppa. They built a diversion dam at about 40th Street and the river. Their first canal ran some three miles in a northwesterly direction. By the spring of 1868 nearly 1,000 acres were in cultivation.

The Swilling Ditch was a grand success and a steady influx of people moved to the Salt River Valley. Other canal companies formed and more farm land opened up each year. Swilling had interests in several canal companies including the Phoenix Ditch, Tempe Canal and Miller Ditch near Mesa.

Around Swilling's farm a small community sprang up called Pumpkinville or Mill City for the Hellings Flour Mill. The prosperous Swilling built the first big house in the

Phoenix area. Swilling Castle, located at 36th Street, had nine rooms and took 96,000 adobe bricks to construct. But Swilling's fortunes were about to change.

In 1871 valley citizens met at McKinnies Saloon and voted to establish the townsite of Phoenix about four miles west of Swillings property. This action enraged Swilling and it's said he shot a man with a double barrel shotgun for voting the wrong way. A citizens committee warned Swilling to mend his violent ways or else. But a year later Swilling "cowhided" a man for slandering a lady. He was brought to trial for assault to commit murder but was acquitted. In 1867 Swilling had killed a man and "in his drunken frenzy had scalped him." Swilling was not a man to cross.

Darrel Duppa, a close associate of Swilling, was happy at the choice of Phoenix. After all he owned land just south of the townsite. Duppa, an educated Englishman, has been credited with giving Phoenix its name. Noting the vanished Hohokam civilization, Duppa predicted a new civilization would rise from the ashes of the old. The Phoenix is the legendary bird of Egypt that is reborn every 500 years from the ashes of its nest.

The job of surveying the townsite of Phoenix fell to Capt. William Hancock. Hancock earned the title Captain in 1866, when he commanded the all-Pima Indian Company C of the Arizona Volunteer Infantry. Hancock's townsite was bounded by 7th Avenue and 7th Street and by Van Buren and Harrison. He built the first house at First Street and Washington, which served as the first courthouse for Maricopa County. Hancock was also the first County Sheriff.

In 1874 Swilling left Phoenix with his wife, Trinidad Escalante, and their five kids and settled down at Black Canyon on the Agua Fria River. Swilling owned several nearby gold mines. But his health was failing. His alcoholism was at a critical stage, and Swilling had another serious problem. He was addicted to morphine which he took to relieve pain from old wounds, including a bullet lodged in his side.

On April 19, 1878 three men robbed the Wickenburg Stage getting $5,000 in gold and silver bullion. During a drunken spree, Swilling boasted that he had done it. Swilling and two pals were arrested. Unable to make bail Swilling was sent to Yuma Prison to await trial. On August 12, 1878 Jack Swilling died in a jail cell at age 48. The charges against his friends were dropped for lack of evidence. It's probable Swilling was jailed because of anger at his drunken tirades rather than serious belief in his guilt. But it was an unfortunate end to a colorful life.

The Territorial Capital moved to Phoenix from Prescott in 1889. For 12 years the Territorial Government occupied the second floor of Phoenix City Hall. In 1901 the new capital building was completed at 17th Avenue and Washington, where the Phoenix street car line ended. The land for the capital had been donated by Moses H. Sherman, the owner of the street car line.

The architect of the capital was James Riley Gordon, who had designed similar buildings in the South. The foundation was malpais rock from Camelback Mountain. The first floor was granite from South Mountain, and the second story was tufa from Kirkland. The capital building was restored from 1974 to 1982, and is now a State Museum. Atop the copper dome sits Winged Victory, a statue that also served as a weather vane. During restoration many bullet holes were found in the statue, confirming stories that cowboys would take target practice at Winged Victory.

The capital has brought Phoenix prestige, power and money. Today thousands of state government jobs help fuel Phoenix's economy. But when Arizona became a

Hohokam artifacts found on early Phoenix farms. Note the large stone axes and shell jewelry including a "thunderbird." The donut shaped stone rings were common, but no one knows what they were used for. *Credit — Author's collection*

state on February 14, 1912, the number of state jobs was quite small. On that first Statehood Day, rotund Governor George W. P. Hunt walked from the Ford Hotel to the capital to celebrate the long awaited event. The famous orator, William Jennings Bryan, spoke to a crowd at the Phoenix City Plaza. That night an inaugural ball was held on the street outside the Adams Hotel.

The Adams Hotel at Central and Adams was not named for its street location but rather for its builder, John C. Adams of Chicago. The original Adams was built in 1896, the most elegant and largest hotel in Phoenix. It stood four stories with a "roof garden" and had shaded porches running around the outside of the hotel. Many hotel patrons used these porches for cooler sleeping during the summer.

The Adams became the "watering hole" for legislators at the state capital. Many out-of-town legislators lived at the Adams Hotel. It's said that copper and cattle barons spent lavish amounts to wine and dine elected representatives at the Adams. Their payoff was legislation favoring their businesses. For some 50 years the smoke-filled rooms of the Adams Hotel was the defacto power center of Arizona lawmaking.

The Adams Hotel was dubbed "absolutely fireproof," but in 1910 the hotel burned to the ground in Phoenix's most spectacular fire. The heat was so intense that firemen a block away from the fire had to shield themselves with wet blankets. A new Adams was promptly built on the ashes of the old. The second Adams took up where the first had left off and resumed the status of Arizona's most powerful establishment. The second Adams Hotel was demolished with explosive charges in the 1970's. It was the first and only building so destroyed in Phoenix. The third Adams Hotel, built on the same site, became the Adams Hilton but was later sold to Sheraton Hotels.

Warm rain fell on mountain snow in the Arizona spring of 1891, and resulted in a gigantic flood sweeping down the Salt River. Much of Phoenix was inundated and many homes were destroyed. Agricultural diversion dams were wiped out as were most canal headings and a number of canals themselves. This flood was ironically followed by a serious drought for the next 10 years. Phoenix experienced an exodus of population for the only time in its history. Farmers sought a more permanent solution to the wet/dry cycle of the Salt River.

The National Reclamation Act was passed by the U.S. Congress in 1902 partly due to pressure from Arizona. The first reclamation project under the new act was approved for Arizona's Salt River. President Theodore Roosevelt said he favored Arizona because he raised most of his Rough Riders regiment here. The main feature of the plan was Roosevelt Dam. At 280 feet, it is the highest masonry dam in the world. When Roosevelt Dam was completed in 1911, a lake with 1,380,000 acre feet of water storage was formed. This provided Phoenix and the surrounding towns with a reliable source for water and a means to control the unstable river.

The Salt River Valley Water Users Association was formed to operate and pay for the vast project. The name was later changed to Salt River Project (SRP). SRP is a unique semi-governmental entity owned by the landowners in the 250,000 acre district. The founders, 1,500 farmers, pledged land as collateral getting one share for each acre. The SRP board was elected by a weighted voting process with each acre allotted one vote. This voting scheme is still in effect today with most homeowners getting a fraction of a vote. It took SRP until 1955 to pay back the $10,166,021 initial loan for the project.

The Salt River Project built five other dams in the succeeding years to increase water storage from the 13,000 square mile watershed. These are Mormon Flat Dam, 1925 (Canyon Lake), Horse Mesa Dam, 1927 (Apache Lake), Stewart Mountain Dam, 1930 (Saguaro Lake), all on the Salt River. On the Verde River SRP built Bartlett Dam in 1939 and Horseshoe Dam in 1946. The money for Horseshoe Dam came in a deal with Phelps Dodge — money for water rights for mining work.

A small amount of hydroelectric power was created with the dams and SRP began selling electricity in the Phoenix area. Today SRP has a share in the Palo Verde Nuclear Power Plant west of Phoenix. Palo Verde is the largest nuclear power facility in the United States.

Agriculture was the Phoenix mainstay for many years. The first boost to farming came in 1887 when the Maricopa and Phoenix Railroad linked up with the Southern Pacific. This opened national markets for local farm products, especially grain and citrus. No commercial citrus was planted in Phoenix before the railroad. World War I created another boom, this time for cotton. The Salt River Valley was called the "Nile Valley of America." Pima long staple cotton replaced Egyptian cotton cut off from markets by the war. In 1920 about 75% of Phoenix area farms were planted in cotton.

Dwight B. Heard was the first major land developer in Phoenix. For three decades, from the turn of the century until his death in 1929, Heard was the undisputed mover and shaker in Phoenix. Heard, born in Boston in 1869, later moved to Chicago and married Maie Bartlett, the daughter of his boss. Her father, Adolphus Bartlett, owned the largest hardware company in the world.

Dwight Heard had lung problems and came to Phoenix in 1895 to regain his health. The Heards liked Phoenix and decided to stay. In partnership with his father-in-law, Heard formed the Bartlett/Heard Land and Cattle Co. The firm bought huge chunks of Phoenix real estate including 7,500 acres in south Phoenix. Heard ran a powerful investment company out of offices at Central and Adams. In 1920 Heard built one of the first "skyscrapers" in Phoenix at that location. This building was still standing in 1989.

Dwight Heard had many influential friends but the foremost was President Theodore Roosevelt. Heard lobbied Roosevelt to get the National Reclamation Act approved and the Salt River chosen for the first project. Both Heard and Roosevelt were part of the Progressive wing of the Republican Party. In 1912 Roosevelt formed the Bull Moose Party and ran for President. To help in Roosevelt's unsuccessful bid, Heard purchased the *Arizona Republican* newspaper. The Heard family controlled the *Arizona Republic* until 1946 when it was sold to Eugene Pulliam of Indiana.

Dwight Heard built his mansion, Casa Blanca, on north Central, just above McDowell Road. This is where the Heard Museum sits today. For 25 years Casa Blanca was the in-spot for Phoenix society and its guest book included names of the most influential and wealthy citizens. Heard owned 160 acres near his home, and this was developed into the prestigious Los Olivas residential area. Other high dollar home developments started by Heard include the Palmcroft Estates near Encanto Park, and Country Club Estates around the Phoenix Country Club at Thomas and Seventh Street.

Maie Bartlett Heard also left her mark on Phoenix. She and Dwight were avid collectors of Indian art. Together they worked to preserve Pueblo Grande and got a municipal museum established there. After Dwight died, Maie continued this work

In 1900 you could fish at Central and Indian School. This carefree Phoenician is atop a cottonwood stump on the Grand Canal. The Grand was dug in 1878 and followed a 1,000-year-old Hohokam canal. The Grand Canal and Arizona Canal are survivors of many ditches that once crisscrossed Phoenix. *Credit — Author's collection*

and established the Heard Museum as a memorial to her husband. In addition Maie donated land for the Phoenix Art Museum and Civic Center in 1940. Maie Heard died in 1951.

World War II brought big changes to Phoenix. Favorable flying weather meant new military air bases for pilot training. Luke and Thunderbird fields were built west of Phoenix. Williams and Falcon fields were established near Mesa. War industries, like AiResearch at Sky Harbor Airport, and Alcoa Aluminum on 35th Avenue, helped sustain a major building boom. One local businessman who prospered on government contracts was Del Webb, who began his construction empire during the war.

However, there were problems. Phoenix had long tolerated a sleazy red light district south of Jefferson Street. Prostitution and gambling were wide open and this naturally attracted military personnel looking for off-duty excitement. But local base commanders declared downtown Phoenix "off limits." Merchants of all types lost business and moves were made to clean up city hall. Heads rolled in the police department and in other city agencies. The military finally lifted the "off limits" order. One leader of the cleanup was attorney Frank Snell, who soon became the leading power broker in Phoenix.

More reforms took place after the war. From 1919 to 1948 Phoenix had some 22 different mayors and 31 different city managers. To create a more stable city government, a group of prominent citizens led by Alfred Knight, formed the Charter Government Committee. Charter selected a slate of candidates who swept the municipal elections of 1949. among the all-Charter council were Mayor Nickolas Udall, councilmen Barry Goldwater, Harry Rosenzweig, and Margaret Kober, the first woman ever elected in Phoenix.

The Charter Government Committee dominated Phoenix city hall for 25 years. Charter candidates won every seat from 1949 until 1971, often by two to one margins. Charter promoted an image of being above politics. Slots were allotted to a woman, Jew, Mormon, Catholic and later to a black or Hispanic. Charter claimed to be bi-partisan but almost all of the Committee, and the candidates, were Republican. No Charter mayors were Democrats. Charter-backed Republicans often went on to higher office, including Barry Goldwater, Governor Jack Williams, and Senator Paul Fannin.

By 1970 Charter Government was becoming less popular. People said Charter was simply a political machine run by the "good old boys" at the Phoenix Country Club. The first to break the stranglehold was Ed Korrick, whose family owned a large Phoenix department store. At the next election in 1973, political maverick Gary Peter Klahr became the second non-Charter councilman.

In 1975 Charter Government collapsed and five of seven elected were independents. The new mayor was Margaret Hance, who had been a Charter councilman. Charter chose someone else to be mayor and Hance bolted to become the first non-Charter mayor in 25 years. Hance was also the first woman mayor of Phoenix, and she went on to be elected for a record four terms. By 1977 Charter did not offer a slate and an era had ended.

Phoenix voters made major changes in city government in 1982. Voters approved a district system with eight councilmen. Previously all six councilmen were elected at large. In 1983, Terry Goddard, a proponent of the district system was elected mayor. Goddard was the first Democrat to be mayor of Phoenix in nearly four decades. The last Democratic mayor before Goddard was Ray Busey in 1946.

Coping with intense heat has always been a part of Phoenix life. The first ice plant in Phoenix was set up in 1879 by S.F. Lount. The facility produced 1,000 pounds of ice a day which Lount at first sold to housewives from a wheelbarrow. Demand for ice made Lount one of early Phoenix's wealthiest citizens. By 1930 there were seven ice plants in Phoenix.

Before air conditioning people found various ways to cool off. Most common was swimming in the river or in one of the countless irrigation ditches that criss-crossed Phoenix. On summer nights everyone moved their beds outside into the back yard. Screened sleeping porches were later put above garages to catch whatever cool breezes were about.

The women and children of well-to-do families left Phoenix from June until September, often staying in San Diego or Long Beach. Outside of Prescott, the village of Iron Springs became summer home for Phoenix's top families in 1900. A railroad stop allowed husbands to spend weekends with their families at Iron Springs and then return to Phoenix for the workweek. Iron Springs is still a Phoenix institution.

Helping cool Phoenix were thousands of large shade trees located along ditches and in irrigated lawns. After World War II, Salt River Project started cutting down these trees and lining ditches with concrete. This action saved water but it destroyed much of early Phoenix's beauty, and significantly increased temperatures.

The first refrigerated air conditioning in Phoenix was installed in the Hotel Westward Ho in 1929. Refrigeration was very expensive and only commercial buildings could afford it. In the 1930's residents built home-made window box coolers. These first evaporative coolers were wood boxes with an electric fan inside. A garden hose dripped water over an absorbent pad in back. The early cooler pads were made of charcoal and later of excelsior (shredded aspen). The poorer families often used thick burlap sacks.

In 1939 Goettl Brothers began building evaporative coolers on the assembly line. Phoenix was called "Cooler Capital of the World." Over 40% of all evaporative coolers in the world were built in Phoenix. By 1957 all new homes were built with duct systems. The late 1950's saw refrigeration compressors come down in price and refrigerated home air conditioning soon became common.

Today Phoenix is the center of a massive "urban heat island." Agriculture peaked about 1950 and since then over 1.2 million acres of Phoenix-area farmland have been developed. Temperatures have increased steadily, especially at night, as asphalt streets and concrete driveways retain daytime heat. In addition tens of thousands of autos and home air conditioners now put heat into the air. Continued growth can only mean that Phoenix will get even hotter.

Since World War II the Phoenix economy has been dependent on defense industries. Today the largest employer is Motorola with 20,000 employees in the Phoenix area. In 1949 Motorola Radio of Chicago opened a research and development plant in east Phoenix on 56th Street. Motorola prospered doing military work during the Korean War and their Phoenix operations expanded greatly. In 1955 the huge plant at 5000 E. McDowell opened. Today this plant is the largest maker of semi-conductors in the world and employs 10,000 people. Other Motorola plants are now located in Mesa, Tempe, and Chandler.

The second largest Phoenix employer is Garrett's AiResearch which is now owned by Signal Oil. AiResearch began in Phoenix building parts for the B-29 bomber from

1942 to 1946. In 1950 they reopened their Sky Harbor plant with a military contract for gas turbine engines. By 1980 AiResearch was the largest manufacturer of gas turbine engines in the world. Today the company employs about 7,000 people.

The first mayor of Phoenix was John T. Alsap, a lawyer and a doctor. He was company surgeon with King Sam Woolsey's Apache hunting expeditions in the 1860's. Later Alsap was legal counsel for pioneer canal companies. He died in 1886. *Credit — Author's collection*

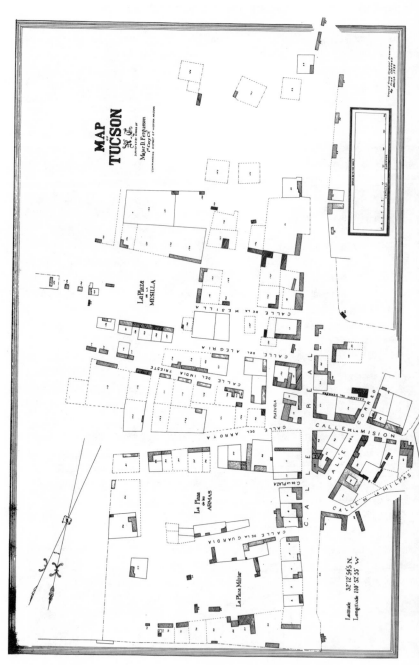

This 1862 map shows Tucson when it was still basically a Mexican frontier town. The buildings around La Plaza Militar and La Plaza de las Armas occupy the original site of the "walled city" founded around 1776. In the early years everyone except local Indians lived inside the 12-foot-high adobe walls of the Spanish presidio.

TUCSON

The Old Pueblo

Tucson, nicknamed the Old Pueblo, is Arizona's oldest and most Mexican city. Once Tucson was a remote outpost on the Spanish frontier and usually surrounded by hostile Apache. Tucson today has high tech industries, a huge Air Force base with nuclear weapons and sprawling urban growth. Yet it retains much of its Indian, Mexican and desert frontier roots.

Tucson is an Indian word that means "place of dark springs" or "springs at the base of a black hill." Over the years it has been spelled many ways including Tuquison, Teuson, Tuczon, Toison, Toixon, Chuk Shon, Frucson, and Lucson. About 1900 "Americans" began to pronounce it "too-sahn." But today Mexicans still pronounce it "took-sone."

The Pima or O'odham Indians have lived here for centuries growing corn, pumpkins, melons, cotton and other crops with Santa Cruz River irrigation water. The Spanish arrived in the mid 1500's and named the region Pimeria Alta or "upper land of the Pimas." The place was so remote, and the native tribes so hostile, that the Spanish left the Tucson Indians pretty much alone until about 1690.

Padre Eusebio Kino founded the Spanish reign in Arizona but he was not Spanish himself. Born in the Austrian Alps in 1645, Kino joined the Jesuits and was sent to Mexico in 1680. Unsuccessful in Baja California, Kino was assigned to Pimeria Alta in 1687. His journal reports 800 Indians were living in 177 houses at Tucson in 1697.

However, Kino built his main Arizona mission at the smaller village of Bac, nine miles south of Tucson. Kino chose Bac because it was the traditional training site for Indian "medicine men." Catholic missionaries often selected places of religious significance to Indians as church sites. This allowed them to suppress the native religion, and to take advantage of established pilgrimage habits.

Resistance to the missions was strong, and Father Kino's efforts were largely symbolic. When Kino died in 1711, his missions in Arizona, including San Xavier del Bac, were without priests. However, Spanish and mixed blood (mestizo) colonists were flocking to the area. Rich silver mines and vast cattle ranches were the lure.

Life was not easy on the frontier. There was the constant threat of Apache raids as well as Pima discontent over losing their best lands. In 1751 the Pima rose up and killed over 100 settlers in Pimeria Alta. To protect colonists, the Spanish then set up the military presidio at Tubac (40 miles south of Tucson) in 1752.

An Irishman, Don Hugo O'Connor, founded the Spanish city of Tucson. O'Connor was one of the "Wild Geese," Irish expatriates who hired out to the Spanish Empire. Assigned to upgrade frontier defenses, O'Connor visited Tucson on August 20, 1775. He saw that Tucson was the main Indian village and ordered the presidio moved from Tubac to the more strategic location. Father Garces was with O'Connor and he designated St. Augustine the patron saint of Tucson.

Capitan Pedro Allande y Saabedra was the first full-time commander of the Tucson presidio. He arrived in 1777 and served until 1786. Allande supervised construction of the walled presidio which was completed in 1783. The new presidio did not halt Apache attacks. A large party of Apache raided Tucson at dawn on March

21, 1784 and killed five soldiers plus stealing 150 horses. Allande led his men against the Apache on numerous occasions. Heads of decapitated Apache warriors were often placed on stakes above the walls of Tucson presidio.

Spanish Tucson was a walled city. Everyone except local Indians lived inside the 12-foot-high adobe walls. The square-shaped fortress was about 750 feet long with small gun towers at the corners. Houses lined inside walls and soldiers used roofs as ramparts. A chapel with cemetery, corrals for livestock, a mescal cantina, a store and well were located inside the walls. There was only one gate (west side) made of massive mesquite logs. From 20 to 100 soldiers were assigned to the presidio. Supplies came from Sonora in caravans of two-wheeled wood carts pulled by oxen.

Dirt for the presidio walls created a ditch, later called Calle de Arroyo. This ditch often filled with water and led to reports that Tucson had a moat. The Pima County Courthouse now occupies the approximate site of the presidio.

The Golden Age of Spanish Tucson was from about 1790 until 1820. San Xavier del Bac Mission flourished and the magnificent church itself was completed by the Franciscan order in 1797. The Apache problem subsided due to punishing military expeditions and other less violent incentives.

Apache bands were issued rations if they came into Tucson and led peaceful lives. In 1793 nearly 100 Arivaipa Apaches settled in Tucson not far from the presidio. In 1819 over two hundred Pinal Apaches came to live in Tucson. This did not make the original Indian residents, the Pimas, very happy and there was conflict between the groups. Called Apache Mansos or Tame Apaches, they often acted as scouts for presidio troops. The "wild Apaches" called them "tontos" or fools.

Mexican Independence brought hardship to Tucson. It began in 1810 with Padre Hidalgo's march on Mexico City and it culminated in 1821 with the Spanish expulsion. Mexican self-determination meant years of chaos. Money for presidio troops and Apache rations dried up. The missions were abandoned including San Xavier del Bac. A period of vicious Apache/Mexican warfare broke out that lasted some 40 years.

On the bright side, Mexican Independence meant home rule. In 1824 the first Tucson mayor, Jose de Leon, was elected. The de Leon family had deep roots in the region. Other significant changes occurred as the first Americans entered southern Arizona. Previously most mountain men stayed in the north where hunting was better. On New Year's Eve 1826 three unidentified American trappers came to Tucson with "passports" issued in Santa Fe.

The United States, after trying to buy California and New Mexico, declared war on Mexico on May 21, 1846. General Kearny took New Mexico with little resistance and then sent the Mormon Battalion to help take California. Col. Philip St. George Cooke led the 500-man Mormon Battalion into Tucson on December 17, 1846 and left the next day. The outnumbered Mexicans under Capitan Antonio Comaduran retreated to Bac. Tucson played no further role in the war.

The 1848 Treaty of Guadalupe Hidalgo ended the Mexican War. Mexico got $15,000,000 and the U.S. got 500,000 square miles of land. However, Tucson remained a part of Mexico until the 1854 Gadsden Purchase. At that time all of Arizona south of the Gila River was bought by the U.S. for $10,000,000. Tucson was now an American town.

Tucson's Congress Street in 1884 was the main business section of town. Several Indian women have come into Tucson to sell large pots carried on their backs. Note the adobe walls behind wooden false fronts. This is typical of how Tucson was changing from a Mexican town to one dominated by "American" styles. *Credit — Author's collection*

Mexican troops stayed in Tucson until late 1856, when the U.S. First Dragoons arrived. Many Mexican families left Tucson with the departing presidio soldiers, but others welcomed Americans. A number of Americans were already living in Tucson. They included Apache fighter and rancher Pete Kitchen, father of Arizona and mine promoter Charles Poston, merchant Mark Aldrich, and John "Pie" Allen who sold fruit pies for $1 a piece.

The First Dragoons were led into Tucson by Major Enouch Steen, who was supposed to establish a military post there. But Maj. Steen found Tucson intolerable, and instead set up Fort Buchanan near Sonoita. Reprimanded for this action, Steen replied that those in Tucson who wanted the troops the most were the sellers of whiskey and women.

When the Civil War broke out all U.S. troops were withdrawn from Arizona. Angry Tucson citizens voted to join the Confederate side. One motive was to get Confederate troops to fight the Apache. Capt. Sherod Hunter with a company of rebel cavalry arrived in Tucson on February 28, 1862. But by May the Confederates fled before advancing Union soldiers recruited in California.

The California Column, 1,800 men strong, was led by Gen. James H. Carleton. In Tucson but a short time, Carleton declared martial law, imprisoned desperados and Confederate sympathizers, and laid a heavy tax on saloons. Carleton left a detachment of troops in downtown Tucson near where the Santa Rita Hotel is today. Only a few buildings were erected — an arsenal and a guardhouse — but Armory Park is a reminder of that period.

In 1872 General George Crook found Tucson "unfit for occupation of animals much less troops." He moved the military post to Rillito Creek about seven miles northeast and established Fort Lowell. In 1891 the post was closed. Today at Fort Lowell there is a museum open to the public.

Graffiti on an abandoned adobe building in Barrio Viejo in Tucson. Note the thick walls and high ceilings that helped keep buildings cool before modern air conditioning. *Credit — Author*

The first stage travel came in the late 1850's with the Jackass Mail and later the Butterfield Overland Stage. Tucson was the main town between El Paso and San Diego. Stages arrived in Tucson four days a week — two heading east and two heading west. But accommodations were primitive at first. Some travelers told a joke about the "Tucson bed" ... "lie on your stomach and cover yourself with your back."

For some newcomers used to better living conditions, Tucson was a shock. In 1865 Mrs. Granville Oury described Tucson as "certainly the most forlorn, dreary, desolate, God forsaken spot on Earth." There were but "two glass windows in the town and not a single board floor."

J. Ross Browne, a journalist with a typically sensational outlook, found Tucson to be "literally a paradise of devils." Browne went on to say ... "Murderers, thieves, cutthroats and gamblers formed the mass of the population. Every man went armed to the teeth. Street fights were a daily occurrence. Men no longer permitted to live in California found the climate of Tucson congenial to their health. The garrison confined itself to getting drunk or doing nothing."

Tucson retained its desperado image into the 1900's. John Dillinger, the "most wanted" bank robber in the 1930's, used Tucson as a vacation spot between robberies. He and his gang were arrested in Tucson in January 1934. A fire at the Pioneer Hotel gave police the tip. Russell Clark, a Pioneer guest, convinced firemen to go back into the burning building and save his unusually heavy luggage. It turned out later the bags were full of Thompson machine guns, pistols, ammo, and bulletproof vests. After the fire a fireman saw Clark's photo in a crime article and contacted police. Clark was spotted and police found the hideout at 927 North Second Avenue. They arrested Clark, two other men, and three girlfriends. Dillinger was not there but police staked out the house and later arrested the gang leader. They were extradited to Indiana but Dillinger escaped. He was later killed outside a Chicago movie theatre in July 1934.

Bank robbers were not the only criminals attracted to Tucson. As early as 1951 mobster Mickey Cohen was looking for business opportunities in Tucson. In 1959 two Tucson men were severely beaten for calling a Mafia chief a "dago." In 1960 a man was shot to death in the apartment doorway of a reputed Mafia leader. In 1969 Newton Pfeffer plummeted to his death from the 11th floor of the Pioneer Hotel. A note said John Battaglia had ruined him. Investigators claimed that Battaglia had taken $4.5 million in jewels from Pfeffer and failed to pay for them.

Fairly or unfairly, Tucson gained a reputation as a Mafia hideaway. Most of the attention focused on Joe Bonanno Sr. and his family in the 1970's. Police sources claimed Bonanno was the dominant Mafia figure in the West. They said he set up the famous French Connection heroin smuggling ring. In Tucson Bonnano kept a low profile in a modest house, but police surveillance was almost round the clock. Police said Bonnano would drive to various public phone booths and spend hours speaking Sicilian dialect to unknown parties.

The second of the Big Two in Tucson's reputed Mafia hierarchy was Peter Licavoli from Detroit. Licavoli was said to have started as a bootlegger with Jewish Mob connections. It's said he was arrested 40 times. In Tucson he lived on the east side at Grace Ranch, supposedly a favorite meeting place for big name Mafiosos. In 1976 Licavoli was convicted of receiving stolen paintings at his Vesuvio Art Gallery at Grace Ranch.

More recently Tucson has been dubbed a major smuggling center for the Mexican Connection — both drugs and illegal aliens. One Tucson Mexican-American who was convicted in 1977 of narcotics violations, was said to be a close associate of the chief of the Sonora State Police. In 1988 five Mexican men allegedly involved in drug smuggling were found murdered in west Tucson.

Another alleged organized crime element in Tucson are biker gangs. Police claim these groups use topless bars as bases for drug dealing and prostitution. The Outlaws, a biker group from Florida, came to Tucson when their leader Big Jim Nolan was paroled there. Big Jim was later jailed for killing a man outside the Bashful Bandit bar. Other notorious Tucson biker gangs include the Mongols, Devils Disciples, Dirty Dozen and Hell's Angels.

The University of Arizona (UofA) has been a source of pride for Tucson but the initial reception was a bit chilly. C.C. Stephens, a Tucson city councilman, was sent to Prescott in 1885 to get the Territorial capital returned to Tucson. Instead Stephens got the university. He tried to explain, but angry citizens pelted him with rotten eggs, spoiled vegetables, and even a dead cat.

The Territorial Legislature appropriated only $25,000 for the university. Tucson was further miffed because Phoenix got the Insane Asylum and $100,000. And Tucson had to supply the land to get the money. No one came forward until the last minute when three local gamblers and saloonkeepers donated 40 acres. The University of Arizona was on its way.

The UofA officially opened on October 1, 1891. It had six professors, 32 students and two schools — Mines and Agriculture. Everything was stuffed into a single building, now known as Old Main. Downstairs were classrooms, library, offices and living quarters for the faculty. The student dorm was on the second floor. In May 1895 three people graduated in the first class.

Over the years the UofA has grown into a major institution with a national reputation. The Agriculture Department was very important in the early years and operated experimental farms at Mesa and Yuma. The Anthropology Department is known for Dr. Emil Haury and his Hohokam excavations. Tree ring dating of archaeology sites was developed at the UofA by Dr. A.E. Douglass. More recently the Optical Sciences Department has earned commendations for work on telescope lenses.

The UofA had the first Law School in Arizona and in 1962 it obtained the only Medical School in the state. It has also gained a reputation as a sports power with strong teams in football, baseball, basketball and other sports. The UofA competes in the Pacific Ten Conference, one of the toughest in the nation.

The UofA campus has several outstanding museums. The Arizona State Museum, built in 1936 with Public Works Administration money, is a Romanesque style brick building with fine collections of Southwest Indian artifacts. The Museum of Art has many rare works. The Center for Creative Photography displays some of the world's best. There is also a fine Mineral Museum at the Geology Department and a Pharmacy Museum at the Medical School.

Today the UofA is the largest employer in Tucson with about 10,000 faculty and staff members and an annual payroll of some $250,000,000. About 35,000 students attend the UofA.

Davis Monthan Air Force Base is Tucson's second largest employer with an annual payroll of $145,000,000 in 1988. It is named after two Tucson natives, Lt.

An old adobe home in Barrio Libre just south of downtown Tucson. This neighborhood has the largest collection of original adobe buildings in the Southwest. *Credit — Author*

Oscar Monthan and Lt. Samuel Davis, who were killed in plane crashes in the early 1920's.

Davis Monthan began as the second Tucson city airport on a section of land (640 acres) bought from the state for a mere $19.50. It was dedicated by the "Lone Eagle," Charles Lindberg in September 1927 — just four months after his historic solo flight across the Atlantic. Lindberg, on a U.S. tour, flew to Tucson in his "Spirit of St. Louis" plane and landed at the old airport on South 6th Avenue. Davis Monthan was the Tucson city airport from 1927 until 1947. The military shared Davis Monthan with the city from 1940 until 1947 when the present city airport was established two miles to the south.

After World War II, Davis Monthan became a storage and disposal site for obsolete planes. This activity continues today but on a much smaller scale. Once it was the world's largest parking lot for old warplanes.

The Air Force expanded Davis Monthan into one of the most sophisticated air bases in the world. For many years it was a front line base for bomber squadrons of the Strategic Air Command. Later the base became regional headquarters for intercontinental Titan II missiles. Armed with nuclear warheads, the Titan II missiles were housed at 18 separate sites surrounding Tucson. Today one missile silo, located near Green Valley, is said to be the only ballistic missile museum in the world.

For many years U-2 spy planes operated out of Davis Monthan despite repeated denials by Air Force officials. City residents often saw the U-2 planes landing and taking off. Davis Monthan has raised the ire of residents of Tucson and nearby communities for years. Aircraft noise and buzzing of homes have been the main complaint. For a while Davis Monthan operated a bombing range just six miles south of Tucson.

Today Davis Monthan is at the forefront of the nuclear weapons controversy. The base is now a major site for the destruction of cruise missiles. The INF Treaty, signed by USSR leader Gorbachev and President Reagan, calls for the demolition of all medium range nuclear missiles. In 1988, Soviet inspectors watched as workmen destroyed 84 cruise missiles. In all, 429 cruise missiles were scheduled to be destroyed at Davis Monthan during a three-year period.

Mission San Xavier del Bac is without doubt the most beautiful Spanish mission church in the U.S. Sometimes called the White Dove of the Desert, San Xavier is located about 10 miles south of downtown Tucson. It is built of white lime plaster over burnt adobe brick.

San Xavier was founded by the Jesuit Father Kino in 1700 but the present church was built by Franciscans many years later. The foundation is probably Jesuit as the Franciscans did not use the cruciform plan in their architecture. In 1783 Father Juan Bautista Velderrain began construction but he died in 1790. Friar Juan Bautista Llorens finished the project in 1797. It is thought the principal builder was Pedro Boroquez. In 1906 Father Granjon extensively remodeled the complex.

Mass is held daily, and there is no admission to the church itself. On the high altar sits a statue of San Xavier that was made in Mexico City in 1759. Nearby on Grotto Hill is a replica of the grotto at Lourdes. The San Xavier Mission was established for the Papago or Tohono O'odham Indians. It still serves the Indian community as their parish church.

The Arizona-Sonora Desert Museum, one of the top zoos in the world, is located in Tucson Mountain Park some 14 miles west of downtown Tucson. The non-profit museum is dedicated to preserving the Sonoran Desert of Arizona, Sonora and Baja California in Mexico. Over 200 animals and 300 plant species are on display.

Tucson retirees William H. Carr and Arthur Pack founded the museum in 1952 to teach conservation. Carr was a former assistant curator at the American Museum of Natural History in New York. Pack was editor and publisher of *Nature* magazine.

The museum is known for naturalistic enclosures, including a 160-foot tunnel for viewing nocturnal animals, a cliff-like bighorn sheep exhibit, a beaver pond with underwater windows and "wildcat" canyons. The realistic wet cave exhibit is also very popular, especially with children. *Sunset Magazine* co-sponsored the Demonstration Garden which shows how native plants can be used in home landscaping. The Earth Sciences Center offers regional geology exhibits. The museum is open every day of the year.

Old Tucson is both a western movie set and a theme park for tourists. It was built by Columbia Studios in 1939 for its epic western "Arizona" which starred Jean Arthur and William Holden. Since then Old Tucson has been the backdrop for over 100 films, many TV shows and countless commercials. Films include "Rio Bravo," "Gunfight at the OK Corral," "McClintock," "Dirty Dingus McGee" and "The Gambler." TV series include "Death Valley Days," "Have Gun Will Travel," "Father Murphy," "Playhouse 90" and "Little House on the Prairie." It is open 365 days a year and charges admission.

The Arizona Historical Society operates a "world class" museum just west of the University of Arizona campus on Park Avenue. An outstanding feature of the museum is a "life-size" mining exhibit with assay office, stamp mill and underground mine. Founded in 1884 by early Arizona pioneers, the Society is also a major research facility for southwest history. Its library contains more than 35,000 hard-to-find volumes and over 250,000 old photographs. Visitors may study these research collections in the Society reading room. There is no admission to the museum.

The Wishing Shrine at Main and Simpson Streets in Barro Libre is an unusual bit of Tucson folk history. Also known as El Tiradito or the "little castaway," it is said to be the grave site of Juan Oliveras. No one really knows when he died or when Mexican women began lighting candles on his grave. But in 1927 the Tucson City Council set out to determine the true origin of the popular shrine.

According to the best available sources, it's believed that Juan Oliveras was killed by his father-in-law sometime in the late 1800's. It is said that Juan was having an illicit love affair with his mother-in-law. When the father-in-law discovered the immoral couple, he took an axe and killed the younger man. Since Juan was involved in an adulterous affair the local priest would not bury him in the church cemetery. Thus he was buried where he was slain.

Local women took pitty on Juan, whom they called El Tiradito, and burned candles for his soul. Folklore grew up that a wish would be granted if a candle burned all night down to the base. Soon many candles were seen at the shrine every night.

The current location of the Wishing Shrine is not the original. It was first located about a block away at Simpson and Meyer streets. When Simpson was extended to Main Street, the shrine and grave were moved to the present site. In 1940 the National Youth Administration built the current shrine with its adobe walls and iron

San Xavier del Bac is located on the Tohono O'odham Reservation about 10 miles south of downtown Tucson. Founded in 1700 by the Jesuit Father Kino, the Mission was completed by Franciscan Fathers in 1797. Mass is said daily and the public is admitted free of charge. *Credit — Author*

candelabras. Some say the new beautified shrine has diminished its power. The old site was described as a rubbish heap strewn with trash where candles were placed haphazardly on a mound of dirt covering the grave. But candles are still burnt for El Tiradito, which creates an eerie mysterious effect when seen at night.

The Wishing Shrine or El Tiradito (Little Castaway) is reputed to have supernatural power. The Shrine is the gravesite of a murdered man denied burial in the Catholic cemetery. Legend says a wish will come true if your candle burns all night down to the base. The Shrine is located at Main and Simpson near downtown Tucson. *Credit — Author*

TOMBSTONE

The Town Too Tough to Die

A sinister place full of crooked gamblers, wicked harlots and brawling miners is how the dime novels portrayed Tombstone. It was a town where whiskey flowed like water and cost about the same as well. Blazing gunfights between vicious outlaws and virtuous lawmen were common, and lynchings were the answer to soft-hearted judges.

This obviously exaggerated portrait has made Tombstone the most famous and most glamorized, silver mining boom town in America. But Tombstone boosters gladly encourage it, because even today tourists flock to the "town too tough to die."

The unlikely town name was chosen by Ed Schieffelin, a non-drinking prospector. Army troops at Fort Huachuca warned Schieffelin not to enter Apache country alone. They told him all he would ever find was his own "tombstone." Schieffelin, a natural loner, disregarded their advice in 1877 and became fabulously wealthy.

Ed Schieffelin is the quintessential prospector who went from rags to riches. An early description said he had "black curly hair below his shoulders, and an untrimmed beard, with unkempt knots and mats. His clothing was covered with patches of deer-skin, flannel and corduroy. His hat was pieced together with rabbit skin." When Schieffelin located the Tombstone and Graveyard claims, he was too poor to pay for assay work and could not determine the value of his ore.

To raise money Ed Schieffelin went to work at the Signal Mine in Mohave County, where his brother Al was employed. The assayer at Signal was Dick Gird, a friend of Al Schieffelin. Gird tested the Tombstone ore samples and promptly proposed a three-way partnership.

In February, 1878 the three men rushed back to the San Pedro River fearing claim jumpers and set up headquarters in an abandoned adobe building. The previous owner had been murdered several years before. Soon they registered the Tough Nut, Goodenough and Lucky Cuss claims and formed the Tombstone Mining and Milling Company. Early assays yielded as much as $15,000 a ton in silver and $1,200 per ton in gold.

A man named Williams was second on the scene and located a mine called the Grand Central. But Williams had originally agreed to share his find. When confronted by Gird, he reluctantly cut off part of the claim and gave it to Tombstone Mining. This claim became known as the Contention, and it turned out to be the richest of all. However, the Schieffelins and Gird sold it cheap for $10,000 to raise operating capital. Eventually other prospectors showed up and some 3,000 claims were filed. Within a year 14 active mines were in operation.

At first the Schieffelins ran the mines while Dick Gird ran the mill and smelter. But Ed Schieffelin soon tired of this and "fled to the hills." In March, 1880 Ed and Al Schieffelin sold their interest in Tombstone Mining for $600,000. A year later Dick Gird sold out for the same amount. Al Schieffelin died of tuberculosis a few years later. Dick Gird moved to California and bought a large ranch which he subdivided into the town of Chino. Gird also became a "sugar beet baron" before his death in 1910.

This is the stylish smelter of the Grand Central Mine with bustling silver-rich Tombstone in the background. Note stacks of cord wood in foreground — fuel for the Grand Central's three boilers. The large building close to town is part of Tombstone Mining, the company that made prospector Ed Schieffelin very wealthy. *Credit — Author's collection*

Ed Schieffelin did enjoy his wealth on occasion, but his real pleasure was solitude. He took up life as a prospector again and roamed the back country. In 1896 he died at age 49 of heart failure at the door of his Oregon cabin, a sack of mysterious ore samples by his side. He left an elaborate will which stated "under no circumstances do I want to be buried in a graveyard or cemetery." His body was dressed in prospector garb with his canteen and pick beside him. A rock cairn used by prospectors to mark their claims was his only monument. Ed Schieffelin is buried three miles west of Tombstone on the site of his first claim.

The Shoot-Out at the OK Corral is Tombstone's most famous event. It's been distorted numerous times on TV and in the movies. Usually the two factions are the Cowboys (Bad Guys) and the Lawmen (Good Guys). It was as much a dispute between Republicans and Democrats.

Wyatt Earp with five brothers and friends like Luke Short, Bat Masterson and Doc Holliday arrived in Tombstone from Dodge City. Most of these men were professional gamblers and hired guns. Virgil Earp was appointed town marshall by Mayor John Clum, a Republican, who also owned the famous *Tombstone Epitaph* newspaper. The sheriff of Cochise County was John Behan, a Democrat. These positions were plums because lawmen doubled as tax collectors and kept a percentage.

The cowboy faction were cattlemen and/or rustlers who lived outside of Tombstone. They included the Clantons (Ike, Phineas, and Billy), Frank and Tom McLowry, Curly Bill Brocius, Johnny Ringo and others. This faction accused the Earps of robbing a stage in March, 1881 and blaming them. Big Nose Kate Elder, who was Doc Holliday's mistress, even swore out an affidavit claiming Doc had killed the stage driver. Virgil Earp arrested Kate, and she promptly moved to Globe. Tensions continued that year.

On October 26, 1881 the Clantons and McLowrys were in Tombstone for supplies. Tombstone outlawed wearing guns, and Ike Clanton and Tom McLowry were unarmed when they argued with the Earps that morning. The Earps pistol-whipped the two cowboys. Later at the OK Corral the Clantons and McLowrys were mounting their horses to leave town. Four heavily armed "lawmen" approached. Wyatt, Virgil and Morgan Earp with Doc Holliday carrying a sawed-off shotgun. Eyewitnesses said Earp yelled "hands up" and immediately began shooting.

Only 18-year-old Billy Clanton and Frank McLowry were armed. Ike Clanton and Tom McLowry had deposited their weapons at the gunsmith shop. Within 20 seconds Billy Clanton, Frank and Tom McLowry were dead. Virgil and Morgan Earp were slightly wounded.

The dead men were buried with a banner "Murdered on the Streets of Tombstone." Tombstone turned against the Earps, and Virgil was suspended as marshall. Sheriff Behan arrested the Earps, but they were brought before Judge Wells Spicer, a Republican, who dismissed the charges. Even the Law and Order faction of the Republicans came out against the killers. Next time there would be no trial, they said next time they would lynch the Earps.

A death list was circulated which included the Earps, Mayor Clum and Judge Spicer. Morgan Earp was killed in ambush while playing pool at Hutch's Saloon. Mayor Clum sold the *Epitaph* and departed the scene. Wyatt Earp left town and abandoned his second wife Mattie Blaylock in the process. Wyatt did stop in Tucson long enough to kill Frank Stillwell. But he fled the state with a murder warrant on his head.

Edward Schieffelin, the prospector who founded Tombstone, is shown with a gun, canteen and rock pick — his basic prospecting outfit. This photo was taken by C.S. Fly after Schieffelin had struck it rich, and purchased an expensive pair of patent leather boots. Before he found his silver mine, Schieffelin was known to wear rags that he patched himself. *Credit — C.S. Fly*

How did Wyatt Earp get his reputation as a Good Guy? Wyatt moved to San Francisco and married Josephine Marcus, a very wealthy woman. She paid to have a favorable biography written. In his later years Wyatt Earp owned saloons in Nevada and Alaska. He also raced horses and generally publicized himself with his wife's money. He died in 1929 at age 80.

Tombstone's wealth attracted more than gamblers and gunslingers. It became a major stop for theatrical troupes on cross country tours. Minstrel shows, magicians, ventriloquists, wrestlers as well as singers, musicians and actors flocked to silver-rich Tombstone.

Schieffelin Hall, said to be the largest adobe building in the U.S., was the place for legitimate theatre. The two-story building had a capacity of 700 and boasted a Colorado mountain scene on its curtain drop. Today it is a community building.

The Bird Cage Theatre, now a popular museum, was the "wickedest night spot between New Orleans and San Francisco" with rowdy burlesque productions. Opened by Billy Hutchinson in 1881, the Bird Cage had a resident troupe of performers who doubled as bartenders and barmaids. Famous vaudevillian Eddie Foy played there and called it "the coffin" due to its size and shape.

One night at the Bird Cage a heckler in a curtained booth harassed the Tombstone Nightingale as she sang. Warned to keep quite, the rude heckler persisted and bouncers were called. A fight broke out and gunshots pierced the air. A body tumbled out of the second floor booth and onto the stage, to the surprised cries of patrons. No problem. It was all a joke planned by fun-loving Billy Hutchinson. The body was a dummy filled with rags. Just good fun in Tombstone.

Another source of entertainment were numerous houses of prostitution located along Sixth Street. Famous madames included Crazy Horse Lil, Madame Moustache, Lizette the Flying Nymph, and Cora Davis, said to be the most honest. Blond Marie was madame of a French girls house which had links to an organized syndicate in France. A French "Count" often came to Tombstone to check on his high-class operation. Blond Marie saved her money and returned to Paris in the 1890's. Prostitution was legal in Tombstone, and a city tax receipt for a "house of ill fame" is on display at a local museum.

Not all Tombstone women had bad reputations. Nellie Cashman was known as the "Angel of Mercy" to miners. Irish Nellie opened a popular restaurant, Russ House, and was the local leader in charity drives. When no Catholic priest was available, Nellie Cashman heard the confessions of men sentenced to hang. She even organized a crew that destroyed a grandstand erected to watch public hangings. Nellie single-handedly raised five children of her deceased sister. Later she followed the Gold Rush to the Klondyke and died in British Columbia in 1925.

By 1886 Tombstone's boom was over. Water was found at the 500 foot level in the mines and silver prices were in decline. Miners moved on to Bisbee or Globe. Only the county courthouse kept Tombstone from complete collapse. The *Tombstone Epitaph* survived by printing legal notices for Cochise County.

A brief rebirth occurred in 1901 when Tombstone Consolidated acquired all the major mines. Huge pumps were installed, and mine works went down to the 1,000 foot level. But in 1909 the second boom was over. In 1914 Phelps Dodge purchased most Tombstone mines for $500,000. Leasees have reopened mines from time to time without much success.

Tombstone lost the County Seat in 1929 to Bisbee. Town boosters feared further collapse and organized Helldorado Week that same year to attract silver-rich tourists. The town's Wild West image was helped by several popular books published about this same time. Boothill Cemetery was "redone," and clever epitaphs were invented for new headboards. Most do not mark known graves, however. Today Boothill Cemetery is a popular tourist stop. The old county courthouse is now a state park museum. Helldorado Week is held every year in mid-October. Each Sunday "gun-fighters" re-enact a fantasy version of the Shoot-Out at the OK Corral.

COLORADO CITY (SHORT CREEK)

Stronghold for Modern-Day Polygamists

Colorado City is an infamous refuge for polygamists excommunicated from the Mormon Church. The town is located right on the Utah border in a remote region north of the Grand Canyon known as the Arizona Strip.

Individual Mormon families began farming Short Creek in the 1860's. But it wasn't until after 1890 that anyone took notice of the place. In 1890 the Mormons (Church of Jesus Christ of Latter Day Saints) decreed polygamy invalid in an effort to win statehood for Utah. Polygamy was widespread in the early Mormon Church.

Fundamentalist Mormons unhappy with the church ban on polygamy began moving to Short Creek. Polygamists liked the location because it allowed them to slip across the stateline into Utah, and vice versa, whenever legal authorities threatened. Hilldale, Utah is directly across the line and shares the polygamist doctrine of their neighbors.

In the 1930's Short Creek saw a heavy influx of polygamists from Utah. In 1935 six Short Creek men were convicted of polygamy. In 1944 the FBI raided the town and arrested several men. But the big raid that gave Short Creek a national reputation occurred in the summer of 1953.

The Arizona Legislature approved $10,000 to investigate Short Creek. The Burns Detective Agency, posing as "movie scouts," made maps of the town and identified houses of known polygamists. Mohave County officials pushed for action citing possible violation of several laws including tax fraud and statutory rape. Governor Howard Pyle declared Short Creek in a "state of insurrection" and secretly mobilized state police and National Guard units for a surprise raid. In the pre-dawn hours of July 26, 1953 a task force of 250 began a two-prong assault on the town. They had warrants for 36 men and 86 women. Lanterns flashing in the cliffs above town warned the polygamists. They assembled in the school yard, but offered no resistance. A total of 263 children were rounded up. A Kingman housewife, acting as police matron, was quoted saying, "they all look exactly alike." Twelve of the wives taken into custody were between 13 and 15 years old.

National Guard units provided food for those detained as well as radio communications. Rathole One was code name for Short Creek, and Rathole Two was Governor Pyle's headquarters in Phoenix. Guard vehicles had painted over insignias to avoid the appearance of a military takeover. But public acceptance of the raid was not forthcoming.

Five busloads of wives and children were sent to Phoenix and placed in foster homes, mostly with sympathetic Mormon families. The men arrested were soon released on bail and finally given one year suspended sentences. All families were eventually reunited. Governor Howard Pyle was defeated for re-election in 1954 and blamed his loss on the unpopular raid. In 1958 Short Creek changed its name to Colorado City.

Today the polygamist practices of Colorado City continue unabated. The population is about 2,000. Another 1,400 members of the sect live in Hilldale, Utah, and at least 3,000 reside in the Salt Lake City area. These fundamentalist Mormons believe only polygamists can enter the highest tier of heaven called the Celestial Kingdom. Females wear long dresses, braid their hair in pigtails and wear sunbonnets. No make-up is allowed and no dates are permitted. Until the mid-1980's no one had TV.

There are no privately owned homes in Colorado City. In 1945 a communal trust was set up called the United Effort Plan. It owns all land in Colorado City (and Hilldale) and "loans" land to individuals to build houses. It is estimated that the United Effort Plan has assets of $60,000,000. Since no one in Colorado City owns property, and households average 20 members, about 50% of residents receive welfare. Mohave County says that fully one-third of all its indigent health care money goes to Colorado City.

Until his death in 1986 at age 98, "Uncle" Roy Johnson was the undisputed leader of the cult. Dissidents say Johnson awarded teenage brides to faithful followers. The average man is said to have two or three wives, but favored males have as many as 10 or 15 wives. Marriages are not recorded to avoid bigamy laws. Girls often learn who they will marry when the man arrives to take them to the wedding. Dissidents claim women are treated like "breeding machines" and are expected to bear a child every year. Girls are allegedly told they will go to hell if they resist or complain.

The Barlow family is said to be the dominant power in town. Newspaper reports in 1987 said the mayor was Dan Barlow (eight wives), the town marshall was Sam Barlow (five wives), and the school superintendent was Alvin Barlow (five wives). The only store was run by Joe Barlow, and his son was assistant fire chief. The only gas station was run by Truman Barlow, and his wife was the only female on the town council.

Outsiders, called "outlanders," often wonder how the town maintains a three to one ratio of females to males (adults). Dissidents claim that many teenage boys are "run out of town." In 1987 William Stubbs filed a $1,000,000 lawsuit alleging the Colorado City police were harassing him to make him leave.

As might be expected, visitors are not welcome in Colorado City.

GUADALUPE

A Bit of Old Mexico

Once known as Yaqui Town, Guadalupe was founded about 1908 by Indian refugees from Mexico. Guadalupe, located between Phoenix and Tempe, remains today a proud ethnic enclave of 5,000 with close cultural and family ties to Mexico.

The Yaqui were renowned warriors whose homeland centered around eight dense villages along the Yaqui River in Sonora. At the turn of the century, wealthy Mexican landowners began taking Yaqui farmlands. Armed Yaquis fiercely resisted this takeover. As a result, the Mexican government rounded up Yaquis and sent them to Yucatan jungles to work in slave-like conditions. Many Yaqui fled to the United States and established several villages in Arizona. Guadalupe became the largest Yaqui community.

Guadalupe was first located along the Western Canal some two miles north of the present town. However the Yaqui were forced off this valuable farmland when a judge ruled it had been improperly homesteaded. The old Yaqui cemetery remains at this site.

The Yaquis then "squatted" on vacant desert land owned by the Federal government. Lucius Zittier, a Franciscan priest working with the Yaquis, wrote to President Woodrow Wilson and finally 40 acres were deeded to the dispossessed Indians. This

This mural on a Guadalupe radiator shop depicts the annual Easter ceremonies performed by Yaqui Indian residents of the town. The Yaqui Temple and Catholic Church are side by side with a Deer Dancer and four "evil" Pharisees in the foreground. No photos are allowed of the rituals. *Credit — Author*

land, called La Cuarenta (The Forty), became the core of Guadalupe. Presbyterian missionary Jenny Biehn later arranged for an additional 100 acres. Eventually Guadalupe grew to some 450 acres.

The town is named for the Virgin of Guadalupe, the patron saint of Mexico. In 1531 the Indian Juan Diego was visited by the dark-skinned Virgin on three occasions. A church, just outside of Mexico City, was soon built. This same location had been an Aztec temple dedicated to a pagan goddess. Due to its Indian origins, the Virgin of Guadalupe became a symbol for Mexico itself. Banners of the Virgin were carried in Mexico's War of Independence. Father Lucius gave a statue of the Virgin to the Yaquis and the town was named in her honor. This statue is now in the Yaqui Temple, next door to the Catholic Church.

Each year during Easter season, Yaqui ceremonial dances are held in the plaza. Yaqui dances blend traditional Indian beliefs with Christian teachings. Some masked dancers represent the evil Pharisees or Fariseos. Other dancers make fun of Mexican or U.S. soldiers. These Easter rites are not performed for tourists. They are an ancient and sacred obligation of the participants. A Guadalupe town ordinance makes it illegal to take pictures or make drawings of these ceremonies.

Over the years many Mexican families joined the Yaquis. Today the town is about 66% Mexican and 33% Yaqui.

Distrust of outsiders is a Guadalupe tradition, some say with good reason. Yaquis feared retaliation from Mexico. Mexicans sometimes did not have proper residency documents. Media people and college researchers sometimes snooped into private lives. In the 1960's a professor got a $500,000 grant from the Defense Department to compare Guadalupe to Vietnamese villages. Suspicion continues today as land developers encroach on Guadalupe.

The Guadalupe Organization or GO was formed to fight local poverty in 1964. GO was patterned after other activist neighborhood groups associated with Sol Alinsky's Industrial Areas Foundation. A seed grant came from the Presbyterian Church. To be members of GO, Guadalupe residents paid $1.50 yearly dues. GO operated a credit union and employment office, and distributed poverty funds. Under longtime director Lauro Garcia, an ASU grad and former school teacher, GO became known as one of the most successful anti-poverty groups in the nation.

During the turbulent Sixties, local conservatives in Maricopa County government saw the Guadalupe Organization as a dangerous radical group. In one bitter struggle in 1969, GO actually turned down $67,000 rather than allow outsiders on its Board of Directors. Maricopa County officials then set up a competing group, the Community Action Agency of Guadalupe, and promptly gave them the $67,000.

This split in Guadalupe politics has continued and even intensified over the years. If Lauro Garcia and GO were for something, the other group, usually led by housewife Anna Hernandez, was opposed to it. In 1975 GO supported incorporation of Guadalupe. Anna Hernandez and her group opposed it. Residents voted to incorporate with 294 for and 216 against — an 83% turnout. But conservative Maricopa County Supervisors continued meddling by stacking the first town council (five to two) with anti-incorporation appointments.

The Guadalupe Organization was still active in the 1980's but its emphasis had changed to economic development. El Tianguis, a bright blue Mexican-style shopping square, was built by GO in 1983 with federal grants. El Tianguis means market

Guadalupe Yaqui Temple

Our Lady of Guadalupe Catholic Church

Richard Nearing © 91

This drawing by Tempe artist Richard Nearing shows the Yaqui Temple (El Templo) and Our Lady of Guadalupe Church in Guadalupe. Yaqui Indian ceremonies are held here during the Easter season.

in Mexico and it was designed by Mexican architect Enrique Guillen. The shopping center offers restaurants and shops with Mexican products but it has struggled to attract merchants and customers. Lauro Garcia III, manager of El Tianguis, playfully referred to it as a "Big Blue Elephant." Dance bands from Mexico often play here on weekends and holidays.

Political squabbling seems to be a way of life in Guadalupe. Many blame "compadrismo" or government by friends and relatives. Guadalupe town council meetings often attract larger audiences than does Phoenix. Recall of council members is common and city managers are frequently fired. Guadalupe Mayor Maria Alvarez even had her car firebombed in 1986. But most problems center around the police department.

At one point Guadalupe had five police chiefs in a two-year period. One police chief, who carried a Uzi machine gun around town, was stabbed by an unknown assailant in 1984. This same police chief was later fired after reports he ordered heroin planted in homes of suspected drug dealers. Four Guadalupe residents sued the town over the planted heroin and were awarded large settlements. Another police chief was fired in 1988. He blamed local drug dealers who were out to get him.

Guadalupe residents, called Guadalupanos, are justly proud of their ethnic heritage. Life has a slower pace here and tradition is more important than growth for its own sake. Despite persistent poverty, many residents are content to remain separate from the rat race of mainstream America. There are more important things in life than money and possessions said a Yaqui man. Guadalupanos do it their way.

SUN CITY

Arizona's Premier Retirement Community

Founded in 1960, Sun City was the prototype retirement community, a place where old is beautiful and the young are banished. Today Sun City is known for curved streets, conservative politics, rabbits on the golf courses, and two car garages where one vehicle is an electric golf chart.

Sun City opened model homes to prospective customers on New Year's Day 1960. The homes were priced from $8,500 to $11,300 for a three bedroom with two baths. Ads touted "Paradise Found" and "Country Club Living." Nearby benefits included military installations (Luke Air Force Base) and schools. Sun City was an instant success and 237 homes were sold in the first three days. Overall sales peaked in 1977 with 20 new homes being sold every day.

Sun City was the brainchild of construction magnate Del Webb. He ignored advice against an elderly-only development. Some said the death rate would exceed new sales and the place would not grow. Although 20 residents die each week on average, growth has not been a problem for Sun City. In 1989 Sun City and Sun City West (founded in 1978) had a combined population of over 60,000 older citizens.

Del Webb, born 1899 in Fresno, California, dropped out of school at age 13. For awhile he played pro baseball but in 1927 Webb came to Phoenix with carpenter tools looking for work. Before long he had his own construction company. By World War II, Webb was building airfields, hospitals and even prisoner of war camps. In 1945 he bought 50% interest in the New York Yankees.

Some people said Del Webb had close contacts with organized crime. He built the Flamingo Hotel in Las Vegas with Bugsy Siegal, reputedly the point man for the Meyer Lansky mob. Bugsy Siegal was later gunned down in Los Angeles. Del Webb, the largest casino operator in Nevada, also owned the Sahara. In addition Webb had interests in banking, airlines, mining and oil. He died in 1974.

To finance Sun City, Del Webb turned to J.G. Boswell, a cotton farmer who owned the land northwest of Phoenix. Boswell had a 49% interest with Webb controlling the operation with 51%. Boswell later sold his share of Sun City back to Del Webb. Today Boswell Hospital is the largest building in Sun City.

Despite Sun City's success there were critics who said that separating old people from young people was not healthy for either group. One of Sun City's first residents was E.A. Britton who won his home in a national sales promotion. But Britton left Sun City and returned home to Eugene, Oregon in 1962 saying he missed children and young people. However, many senior citizens clearly preferred to live with other elderly people. Today the only people under 50 regularly seen in Sun City are either gardeners, domestic help or store employees.

No one under 18 years of age may live in Sun City for more than 90 days. So says a zoning restriction enforced by Maricopa County with a $750 fine and four month jail sentence. In addition at least one person per household must be 50 years or older. The Sun City Homeowners Association helps maintain these deed restrictions since Sun City is unincorporated. Complaints usually stem from grandparents helping care for their underage grandchildren. Exceptions to the rule are not tolerated.

Politically Sun City is a conservative power base with 75% of registered voters listed as Republicans. Turnout on election day is usually 90%. GOP fundraisers say Sun City residents give the Republican National Committee the highest rate of contributions in the U.S. But Sun City Union Club, with members like I.W. Abel, former president of the Steelworkers, has tried to rally Democrats.

Sun City voters have repeatedly defeated bids to incorporate their town. In December 1964 voters rejected incorporation by 2558 to 1036. Opponents feel taxes are lower with county services picking up law enforcement duties and road maintenance.

In 1974 Sun City was allowed to withdraw from local school districts. This was done with mutual consent of nearby school boards since Sun City had consistently defeated all school bond elections. As a result Sun City residents pay only 30% as much property tax as surrounding areas.

On the surface Sun City is a very wealthy place. At one time there were 55 bank branches here with assets over $2 billion. Income levels are far higher than retired people as a whole. But even in Sun City there are economic problems. Over 10% of single households had incomes of $6,000 or less per year. Loneliness and boredom are major concerns.

Sun Citians like the theme older and active. There are eight recreation centers, 16 golf courses and 400 civic organizations and clubs. Major groups include the Sun City Taxpayers Association, the Sun City Posse which mans six patrol cars and cruises the streets 24 hours a day, and the Sun City Pom Pons who dance for audiences across the nation. Other clubs include the Circumnavigators Club, the Puppet Club and the Power Riders (motorcycle enthusiasts).

The favorite form of transportation in Sun City is the non-polluting electric golf cart. These homes are the original 1960 models which sold for $8,500 to $11,000. Desert landscaping, with cacti and colored gravels or pebbles, account for 90% of all single family yards in Sun City. *Credit — Author*

BISBEE

The Billion Dollar Copper Camp

The greatest of the Western mining towns, Bisbee was called the Billion Dollar Copper Camp. When the mines closed down in 1975, Bisbee had produced over six billion dollars worth of ore — mostly in copper but also huge amounts of gold and silver. Though the mines are shut down, Bisbee remains a lively community with the county seat (Cochise) and a small tourism industry.

An Army scout, John Dunn, traveling through the Mule Mountains in 1877 was the first to stake a claim here. Dunn returned to Fort Bowie and revealed his find to an alcoholic prospector named George Warren. Warren and his buddies rushed to the spot and located several mines including the incredibly rich Mercey, later renamed the Copper Queen. Although Dunn grubstaked Warren, he never listed Dunn on the claims — a dishonorable oversight in the eyes of many mining men.

Fate was not kind to George Warren. He lost or sold all of his mining property within a few years. In a drunken wager Warren bet he could outrun a horse in a short race. He lost one ninth share of the Copper Queen — estimated worth $20,000,000. Warren was declared insane in 1881 but soon released. He hung around Bisbee getting a small pension from the Copper Queen and doing odd jobs. Buried first in a pauper's grave, Warren's body was exhumed in 1914 and given a monument befitting the "Father of the Camp." Warren is immortalized in the original State Seal of Arizona, his photo was the model for the miner.

Founded in 1880, the town was named for Judge Dewitt Bisbee of San Francisco, a big financial backer of the Copper Queen. It's said Bisbee never set foot in the town that bears his name.

Dr. James Douglas, the "Professor," was an agent for Phelps Dodge Mining of New York. Impressed with Bisbee's potential, the Professor had Phelps Dodge buy the Atlanta Mine adjacent to the Copper Queen in 1881. No high grade ore was found at first. Finally an expensive 200-foot shaft was sunk and a "glorious body of ore" was discovered. The Copper Queen hit the same ore body about the same time. The two companies fought over rights. Eventually Phelps Dodge bought out the largest Copper Queen partners and large scale production began.

The Irish Mag, the second largest mine in Bisbee, was named for a local dance hall girl who paid the claim registration fee. Owned by one James Daley, the Irish Mag sat atop a rich ore body of immense size just south of Copper Queen. James Daley, described as a morbid sort, refused many lucrative offers. Frustrated, the big mining interests used local police to harass Daley. Deputy constable Dan Simon had a little "shoot out" with Daley and the Irish Mag owner spent 1 year in Yuma Prison. Daley vowed never to be arrested again. When W.W. Lewther came to do just that, James Daley killed the lawman and disappeared. His Mexican widow sold the Irish Mag to Tombstone saloon keeper Martin Costelle for $1,800. Costelle turned around and sold the mine to Calumet and Arizona Mining Co. for $550,000. Starting in 1899 Calumet made many millions before merging with Phelps Dodge in 1931.

The most famous event in Bisbee history is the Deportation of 1917. World War I was a turbulent time in Arizona mine towns. Copper prices were high and unions

This is Bisbee soon after the mine was discovered in 1878. Note the "glory hole" above the two-story building. It is still visible today. From these humble beginnings Bisbee grew to be the largest town in Arizona with some 20,000 people in 1920. *Credit — Author's collection*

demanded better wages and safer conditions. Two thousand Bisbee workers went on strike on June 26, 1917. There were also strikes in all other Arizona copper towns. The big mine companies claimed the strikes were really a German plot to stop copper production. John C. Greenway, general manager of Calumet (with others), organized the Workmen's Loyalty League and set about to rid Bisbee of "undesirables."

In the early morning hours of July 12, 1917, Sheriff Harry Wheeler deputized 2,000 armed men and began a house to house search for "troublemakers." Some 1,500 men were rounded up and held in the Warren ballpark. About 300 were released after pledging "loyalty." But 1,186 men were packed onto cattle cars of Phelps Dodge's El Paso and Southwestern Railroad. The train was dubbed the Wobbly Special referring to the Industrial Workers of the World (IWW), nicknamed Wobblys, who were active in the strike. The deportees were taken to an Army camp near Columbus, New Mexico where some of them stayed until September. They were free to go almost immediately but some hoped for favorable legal action and punitive damages. Sheriff Wheeler and others were tried on kidnap charges but acquitted after lengthy trials and appeals. The Loyalty League and kangeroo courts ran Bisbee for a period and bitter feelings lingered for decades. Reportedly no one remotely associated with the Loyalty League ever held office again in Bisbee.

Only two men were killed in the Deportation. Orson McRae was a shift boss at the mine and a Loyalty League officer. McRae burst into the home of James Brew and found the miner still in bed. Brew shot and killed McRae, and Brew was then killed by other Loyalty Leaguers.

Big Daddy, nickname for Phelps Dodge Mining, consolidated its power in Bisbee by absorbing other companies and buying up property. Big Daddy came to own 90% of the land in Bisbee. Today major downtown buildings include Phelps Dodge General Office (1895), now the Historical Museum, Phelps Dodge Mercantile (1939), now closed, the YMCA (1903), built by Phelps Dodge and now the local Recreation Center, and the Copper Queen Hotel. Built by Phelps Dodge in 1902, the Copper Queen is the oldest non-resort hotel in Arizona. Teddy Roosevelt and Gen. Black Jack Pershing were once guests. In 1972 Phelps Dodge sold the hotel to Steve Hutchison, a "newcomer" who restored the old inn and kept it open.

Bisbee may have been the richest copper deposit in the world but high grade ore was not inexhaustible. Low grade ores necessitated opening the huge Lavender Pit surface mine in 1951 where the Irish Mag once stood. Despite the pale purple colors of the Pit, it was named for Harrison Lavender, Phelps Dodge Mine Superintendent. Using huge electric shovels and a fleet of 65-ton trucks, over 350 million tons of rock were removed. The 1,000-foot-deep Pit ate up Sacramento Mountain and much of the town of Lowell before closing in 1974. The Copper Queen Mine, with over 150 miles of underground railroad, closed its doors in 1975 but has now reopened for tours.

As Bisbee's copper industry declined a new phenomena occurred. Newcomers were attracted to Bisbee for cheap housing and an alternate lifestyle. Often described as "hippies" these new arrivals liked the historic setting and casual small town atmosphere. "Arizona's only open air insane asylum," said one recent immigrant. Naturally there was some conflict between the newcomers and oldtimers. One time mayor and city councilman Frank Peters has often been at the center of the conflict. Peters, a restaurant owner, came in 1973 and has waged many campaigns on issues ranging from voter registration to opposing commercial development.

Miners are unloading waste rock from ore cars at the "Billion Dollar" Copper Queen Mine in Bisbee. The mine no longer produces copper but visitors can now tour part of the underground workings. *Credit — Les Barrett*

Around 1920 Bisbee (and its suburbs) was probably the largest city in Arizona with about 20,000 people. It has decreased ever since. In 1959 Bisbee annexed outlying communities including Warren, Lowell, San Jose, Tintown, Saginaw, Galena, Barkerville, Don Louis, Briggs and Huachuca Terrace. Official 1950 census showed 3,801 residents of old Bisbee. In 1960 Bisbee had 9,914 people thanks to annexation. But in 1980 only 7,100 people called Bisbee home. Although tourism was touted as a replacement for mining, it accounts for only about 10% of city income today.

The author is seen here at the entrance to the Queen Mine in Bisbee after touring a portion of the extensive underground workings.

The Copper Queen Hotel (white building) was built for well-heeled Bisbee visitors by the Phelps Dodge Mining Co. Early guests included President Teddy Roosevelt and Gen. Black Jack Pershing. Today it is privately owned and still open to the public. The bar is a hangout for tourists and locals. *Credit — Author*

Index

Bibliography

Bancroft, Hubert Howe. *History of Arizona and New Mexico 1530-1888.* Albuquerque: Horn and Wallace 1962.

Barnes, Will C. *Arizona Place Names.* Tucson: University of Arizona 1960.

Cline, Platt. *They Came to the Mountain.* Flagstaff: Northland 1976.

Crowe, Rosalie (Ed.). *Early Yuma.* Flagstaff: Northland 1976.

Crampton, C. Gregory (Ed.) *Sharlot Hall on the Arizona Strip.* Northland 1975.

Faulk, Odie B. *Tombstone Myth and Reality.* Oxford University Press 1972.

Grattan, Virginia. *Mary Colter — Builder Upon Red Earth.* Flagstaff: Northland Press 1980.

Harte, John Bret. *Tucson — Portrait of a Desert Pueblo.* Tucson Chamber of Commerce 1980.

Hawkins, Helen. *History of Wickenburg to 1875.*

James, Harry. *Pages of Hopi History.* University of Arizona 1974.

Johnson, G. Wesley Jr. *Phoenix Valley of the Sun.* Tulsa: Continental Heritage Press 1982.

Love, Frank. *Yuma's Naughty Past.* Colorado Springs: Little London 1981.

Malach, Roman. *Oatman.* Kingman 1975.

Murbarger, Nell. *Ghosts of the Adobe Walls.* Los Angeles: Westernlore Press 1964.

Odens, Peter. *Dick Hall of Salome.* Yuma: Southwest Printers 1972.

Officer, James E. *Hispanic Arizona.* University of Arizona 1987.

Patton, James. *History of Clifton.* 1977.

Peterson, Charles. *Take Up Your Mission.* University of Arizona 1973.

Sargent, Charles. *Metro Phoenix.* 1988.

Rose, Dan. *Ancient Mines of Ajo.* 1936.

Sheridan, Thomas. *Los Tucsonenses.* University of Arizona 1986.

Smith, Cornelius. *Fort Huachuca.* 1978.

Snowflake Centennial Committee. *Life and Times of Snowflake.* 1978.

Sonnichsen, C.L. *Tucson — Life and Times of American City.* Norman: University of Oklahoma 1982.

Sonnichsen, C.L. *Billy King's Tombstone.* University of Arizona 1972.

Wagoner, Jay. *Arizona's Heritage.* Santa Barbara: Peregrine Smith 1978.

Wilson, Elfred etc. *Arizona Lode Gold Mines and Gold Mining.* Tucson: Arizona Bureau of Mines — University of Arizona 1967.

WPA Writers Program. *Arizona — A State Guide.* New York: Hastings House 1940.

Young, Herbert. *Ghosts of Cleopatra Hill.* Jerome Historical Society 1964.

Zarbin, Earl. *The Swilling Legacy.* Phoenix: Salt River Project 1978.

The following appeared in the *Arizona Gazette* (Phoenix) on June 13, 1882.

Missouri Republican — A Deputy U.S. Marshall who took a hand in the recent collision with the riotous cowboys at Tombstone, Texas has been ambushed and filled full of buckshot. He threatens to get well and have his turn all in good time.

Fort Worth Advance — The *Republican* had better consult its map before it again utters such slanders against Texas. Tombstone is in New Mexico, and is nearly as far from the settled portion of Texas as it is from Missouri. The fact is it was some quiet peaceable Texas boys who were killed in the riot mentioned by the *Republican*.

The Advance man is a geographical scholar, as his correction of the *Republican* illustrates. For our part we know that Tombstone is neither in New Mexico nor Texas. We believe it is located somewhere in Ireland.